IT'S
YOUR
CHOICE!

IT'S YOUR CHOICE!

A PRACTICAL GUIDE TO EMOTIONAL HEALTH

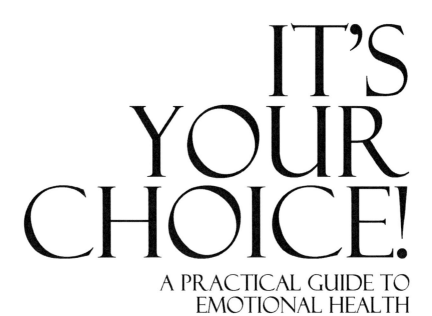

Lee Braddock, MA, CTACC

Outskirts Press, Inc.
Denver, Colorado

"OUR DEEPEST FEAR IS NOT THAT WE ARE INADEQUATE. OUR DEEPEST FEAR IS THAT WE ARE POWERFUL BEYOND MEASURE. IT IS OUR LIGHT, NOT OUR DARKNESS THAT MOST FRIGHTENS US. WE ASK OURSELVES, WHO AM I TO BE BRILLIANT, GORGEOUS, TALENTED, FABULOUS? ACTUALLY, WHO ARE YOU NOT TO BE? YOU ARE A CHILD OF GOD. YOUR PLAYING SMALL DOES NOT SERVE THE WORLD. THERE IS NOTHING ENLIGHTENED ABOUT SHRINKING SO THAT OTHER PEOPLE WON'T FEEL INSECURE AROUND YOU. WE ARE ALL MEANT TO SHINE, AS CHILDREN DO. WE WERE BORN TO MAKE MANIFEST THE GLORY OF GOD THAT IS WITHIN US. IT'S NOT JUST IN SOME OF US; IT'S IN EVERYONE. AND AS WE LET OUR OWN LIGHT SHINE, WE UNCONSCIOUSLY GIVE OTHER PEOPLE PERMISSION TO DO THE SAME. AS WE ARE LIBERATED FROM OUR OWN FEAR, OUR PRESENCE AUTOMATICALLY LIBERATES OTHERS."

~Marianne Williamson~

I dedicate this book to my wonderful wife and best friend, Nan, and to all my clients who supported my efforts and encouraged me to write this book.

Contents

Chapter 3

Chapter 4

Chapter 5

Acknowledgements

I want to thank my beautiful wife, Nan, for her love and devotion who stuck by me and has loved me unconditionally, which enabled me to accomplish all that I have in my life. I would also like to thank Dr. Bruce Pelon and Dr. Ann Michener for their encouragement and validation and Dr. Linda Chamberlain for her encouragement and guidance during my graduate program at Regis University.

These individuals unknowingly influenced me to write this book with an open mind and heart and to care for the people with whom I work. These individuals taught me by example, to respect one's reality and to provide unconditional guidance so that others might achieve a life of self-empowerment and happiness. Thank you all from the bottom of my heart. I pray I can pay it forward with the same grace and commitment as was offered to me.

Lastly, I offer my deepest appreciation and thanks to God for His great love and guidance in the writing of this book.

Foreword

"Changes start when you can see the next step."
~ Unknown Author~

As a psychotherapist, I love what I do for my clients and the people I casually meet in my daily life; I love the interaction with them. Most of all, I take enormous pleasure in watching them grow into strong independent individuals. I would like to share with you some of my experiences and relate the use of tools and techniques that I not only live by, but also teach.

I think it only fair to share with you a bit of my background so you can get a clear understanding of why I am committed to helping people. It is important to know that I do not point fingers or place blame onto anyone or anything. Pointing fingers and placing blame only exacerbates problems to an uncontrollable state. I believe that by examining and developing a clear understanding of the facts, we can create solutions.

My mother did the best she could with the knowledge and life experience she had. Do I agree with some of what she did or how she did it…? Not really! Did I learn from it to better myself…? Yes, absolutely!

Unwittingly, I was raised to feel inadequate, stupid, and incapable of doing anything meaningful or productive in my life. I received no validation or encouragement from my family or teachers. I hated school because I constantly overheard teachers conversing with one another about how stupid and incapable they thought I was in reading and in math. They made comments that they believed me to be retarded. This term was often used during my childhood to indicate someone being inept or mentally slow. However, I found out much later in life that my educational problems were the result of a learning disorder called, dyslexia. Being an individual and having an identity did not appear to be a consideration in my family. Education was not a high priority.

The first time I quit school was when I was in the 8th grade, with no rebuttal from my parents. In fact, my mother agreed with this decision, which was based on an experience I had while attending a small country school in Arkansas. I was having difficulty assimilating and the school had no books to give me. After many requests, I was told by the Principal to find what I needed in the lockers of others. I refused to take someone else' books, and I guess if the truth were known, this was the perfect excuse I needed to quit.

I began smoking and drinking before I reached 12 years of age. At 16, I was smoking openly and regularly with no rebuttal from my mother, as if she gave her consent. My mother will never be accused of being overly sensitive, or touchy-feely. Although I love my mother, she had experienced several marriages during my childhood, all of which were physically or emotionally abusive. She married for the fourth time while I was still living at home, which was not the friendliest or the most loving atmosphere I have ever endured. As for being educational, it certainly was, however, it was not the type of education I would wish on anyone. It was physically and emotionally abusive. I felt I had to walk on egg shells most of the time. I learned to hate and to be angry, and in some cases, I became violent. I learned to dislike women, and I learned how to be a loner. The only relationships I had in school were with one or two friends that I hung around with. As for relationships with girls, my mother attempted to arrange those, but I never really had any. I never had a real date until after I left home and those were rocky at best. I found that I picked all the wrong types. I picked girls that were self-serving and selfish. I got hooked up with two girls that had me beaten up just for their own excitement.

I soon realized that I was fearful of responsibility, unsure of my decision-making processes, and hated to think I was going to have to live life as a complete and total failure. Being a failure was thrown in my face regularly. My life's dream was only to be a great parent and husband. I seemed always to be "drastically unsuccessful" in these areas.

I found myself in arguments and sometimes-physical confrontations while defending my point of view, my beliefs, and my ideologies. I pushed people away emotionally. I drank to reduce my feelings of embarrassment and inadequacy and to deaden the feelings of hatred I felt for myself and others. I felt as though I was so far down on the list of humanity, there was no light at the end of the tunnel. My life was filled with discouragement, guilt, shame, fear, and failure; these feelings eventually grew into self-loathing.

Between the ages of 8 and 15, I was a cutter. A cutter is someone that cuts on themselves as a form of punishment on themselves. People were always willing to offer negative criticism and judgments, but no one was ever willing to explain or offer understanding, as to "why" I was going nowhere or how I could start pulling myself out of this turbulent and hurtful lifestyle. It seemed that everyone I met had inconceivable amounts of disparagement but no positive or constructive advice.

All of my siblings walked away from our childhood with different levels of dysfunction. I would estimate these levels range from a suicidal level on one extreme, to narcissism and emotionally mean and self-serving on the other. Our individual relationships varied in dysfunction, but all ended in divorce at the minimum. The family's basic world view was simply to work and survive at any cost. I soon believed that I had no hope in life. For some unknown reason, I somehow clung to a flimsy hope that I might have a chance for a better life.

I experienced a divorce that created huge resentments and put distance between me and my children. This continues to break my heart almost daily, even after 25 years. My ex-wife informed me on several occasions that she would make sure my relationships with our children would be destroyed…and she succeeded.

If you are having similar experiences as this, I truly empathize with you. This book will assist you in making some very important changes in your life.

I remarried in 1984 and eventually, through her loving spirit, my wife taught me about the true concept of love. Her example demonstrated to me how to freely experience love as well as how to express those feelings. This change took place in me because she showed me, through guidance, and effective communication, instead of simply telling me! I often ask my wife why she stuck it out with me, and she replies with the same answer each time, "I saw goodness in you." I asked her how, and she replied, "I have always had this curiosity to understand why people do what they do." I found her not only to be honorable, but extremely caring for people in general. This demonstrated to me how much I still needed to learn and instilled in me a strong desire to learn more.

Eventually, my wife and I discovered my youngest daughter had dyslexia and that this disorder was inherited from me. The realization of this answered many questions of long ago and struck a chord of curiosity in me. I began to wonder now… "was I really as stupid as I was led to believe?"

When I look back at the problems I experienced throughout my younger life and the problems my children had been experiencing, I realized that *my* history had become *their* history. What a horrible legacy for my children and their children to have.

I found that one's **"History does repeat itself if you don't change your future!!"** People do live what they learn! A history filled with frustration, confusion, despair, and broken dreams followed me throughout my life until I decided to change my future past. A broken family is not simply a divorce between a man and woman. It is the devastation that children are imposed to live with for the rest of their lives because they were wrongfully sucked into the nightmare.

In this book, I offer some highlights of my past and my current life. These tools and techniques combined with making a pledge to change and commit myself to the process have resulted in a greatly improved life and wonderful relationships. My client's lives, as well, have improved.

I hope this book will entice people to take a deep look inside themselves and possibly relate to some of my experiences. May you find the courage to utilize this information to bring about your own self-empowerment for a happier and more fulfilling life. It is a well-known fact that everyone has problems, some worse than others, but what separates one person from another is how they deal with those problems. I have found it very difficult to live in a volatile relationship with anyone. If you commit to developing a happy, healthy relationship with yourself, you have won half the battle.

I don't like using a lot of "psychobabble" or terms that people don't clearly understand. It confuses the real issues of life, and life is confusing enough. I believe if things are simply stated, they will easily be understood and one's willingness to learn is increased. I have attempted to write this book in such a way that anyone can understand. Anyone can apply these techniques to their life. You will find that I repeat many of the tools and techniques, because they are all intertwined. As a dyslexic, I found that repetition increases one's memory.

Throughout this book, I will be asking some important questions that need to be analyzed by you, to help guide you through your life journey. I will offer suggestions and ask you to do home-work, which will help move you to the next level. Regardless of what you have learned, your life and relationships are priceless, so might I suggest that you treat them as such. I truly hope that you enjoy the information.

Thank you and good luck.

How to use this Book

If you are reading this book, I congratulate you on your decision to investigate information that when used regularly can develop into a happier and healthier lifestyle!

The reason I wrote this book is because many of my clients, my wife and friends suggested I put this life changing information into words so that it is available to everyone who wants it. There are many self-help books out there; however, the information in this book is used to teach abuse victims, addicts, couples, and others needing relationship help. If used correctly, it will improve their lives with **great results**.

Much to my chagrin, this information is not taught in schools, churches, or anywhere else within our society. Children are left up to their own devices to learn this information. Most people acquire this knowledge on the streets and do so incorrectly. I have attempted on several occasions to introduce a course into elementary schools, junior colleges, and adult education programs. I have been turned down because the institutions say, "No one wants this stuff," or "this type of class doesn't pay." I only wished the educational system would realize how vitally important this material is and once implemented, teaches people how to live in a happier and healthier life. I truly believe the more people who become self-empowered using the tools and techniques in this book, the fewer problems people and families will experience. These are not simply tools and techniques, they are individually creating healthier lifestyles.

I am so passionate about the information contained in this book, I feel as though I have become somewhat obsessed. I feel a need to share this with everyone desiring to live in a happier and healthier life. I am constantly drawn to help people, and to teach these things because I know they work. I have personally used these tools to change my life and my relationships, and I continue to use it today. If you take this journey, it will not be easy, but if you have the desire and commitment, you will succeed. When I speak to groups, I become like the energizer bunny... I just go on and on and on, and on...and my time management escapes me.

One thing that frustrates me about many self-help books, therapists, and seminars is they all talk about tools and toolboxes; however, rarely do they explain what they are and how to use them or personalize them for individual growth. What I am saying is that we arbitrarily use words and phrases without considering that each of us has our own interpretation and understanding of what is being said.

Everything in this book begins as a concept or an idea. When you arrive at a clear understanding of how to apply a concept or idea in your personal life, these are referred to as techniques. When you finally commit to using these techniques, they become your tools and after sometime using them daily, they will become a lifestyle.

Your toolbox is your heart. Your brain is where you store, embrace, nurture, and own your tools. When you need a tool, you go to your brain, choose the correct tool for the right application, and use your heart to temper the use of that tool.

The way you use this book is to take each concept and consider how it applies or fits into your personal situation. There are questions and assignments that need to be answered and completed to get the full experience. I strongly suggest that you answer all the questions. Start by writing down some short and long-term goals to refer to later. These goals do not have to be sealed in concrete. By writing them down, you do two things. First, you have created a record you can reference often. Second, the deeper you get into this book, the more you might find a need or desire to change those previous writings. I want to stress that you need to be as honest with yourself as possible. Do not justify, rationalize, or intellectualize your thoughts, beliefs, and behaviors.

Examine what issues you need to repair or change in your life that will facilitate the achievement of your goals. This process is referred to as Self-awareness. Write these issues down, as well. I strongly advise you to journal everything, so you can go back for review, to measure and hold yourself accountable for your progress. Examine these concepts to see how they apply in your area of concern.

By learning the concepts in this book, you'll need to develop a written plan of action for yourself. The application process will become difficult as you begin to see where you need to put your personal reciprocal boundaries, and start to enforce them.

By journaling your progress, you'll see how you are advancing and may find that you need to make alterations, so be flexible in planning your goals. This will do much for your confidence, self-esteem, and your commitment. You should create a reward system for yourself or a system of self–recognition and validation for your progress. If you find you are not moving as quickly as you'd hoped, that's okay. Don't push it! Allowing things to occur naturally will ensure a more complete understanding of the concepts.

At some point, you will come to a crossroad. That crossroad will be either indecision or confusion as to what to do. You may need to ask yourself, **"Do I want to be right, or do I want to be happy?"** If you choose to be right, you may rationalize and justify your current existence, and your painful life, and you will remain status quo. If you choose to be happy, you'll make the right decision, regardless of the difficulty. By choosing to be happy, you will find it easier to make a commitment and follow through! What a wonderful way of life.

Note: It is impossible to be right all the time, but we can be happy most of the time. Which would you prefer?

The reason I am so passionate about these tools is I have seen what it has done for my wife, my clients, and for myself. I have witnessed the positive effects it has had on my clients. Again, this is not an easy process. It takes a great deal of work, determination, and a strong personal commitment to self.

I don't believe in telling people what to do. If you have U.S.A. (Unconditional Self Acceptance) and have your reciprocal boundaries in place, you will never feel the need to tell anyone what to do. You will allow them to decide as to whether they want to accept and use the tools offered. This allows people to take control of themselves and their lives. If you set and enforce your reciprocal boundaries, you will feel personally empowered, because you'll know you have ultimate control over your life. My best wishes and hopes for you and your success is to achieve everything you need out of life.

Lastly, your ultimate goal is to become self-empowered. In order to accomplish this, you first need to gain U.S.A., which in itself is a lifestyle.

The other concepts talked about are needed to help you to accomplish your goals. To help to learn to set and enforce your reciprocal boundaries, effective communication, assertiveness, anger management, and developing decision-making skills, etc. There are many other parts to this goal, such as identifying those negative behaviors that keep you down; for example, your destructive self-talk, cognitive distortions, entitlements, unfair expectations, and much more. Keep in mind that this book is intended to teach you what you need to know to regain your identity and individuality, increase your self-esteem and self-worth, and become that happy, healthy, loving person that we all know you are.

Thank you and good luck.

"Self-Empowerment is the act of taking control of your life and success."

~Lee Braddock~

CHAPTER 1

Self-Empowerment

Self-Empowerment is a fascinating concept. It is important to understand what that means for you as an individual, for your relationships, and your families. I believe *"understanding"* is a major key to our existence. If you come to a good, logical, and a clear understanding about what your issues consist of, then you're more empowered to fix them.

Before we get started, consider what you personally want to achieve from this book and what commitment you are willing to make to get it. Write these down so you can refer to them often and be reminded what you are going to do to become successful. Here are some things to consider. Are you or have you ever been in a physically and/or emotionally violent relationship, either as a child or as an adult?

Do you want to gain self-empowerment and personal strength to achieve independence, emotional freedom, and to regain that special gift of your identity?

Do you want to grow within so you can pass down good, solid, workable skills, tools, and techniques to your children? Think for a moment, do you want to create a more complete, happy, and healthy existence for yourself, your children, and your relationships?

The greatest gift God gave to us is the freedom of choice to become who we want to be. Then He gave us our spouse and our children. The greatest gifts we can give them are a happy and healthy example and proper guidance to achieve their own happy life, which I might add, should be the goal for completing your legacy.

Question: Please consider this very seriously... If you were to pass away today, how do you want your family, friends, and children to remember you and refer to you? Your response can be anything from one sentence to a whole volume in length. The reason I want you to think about this is because we all leave a legacy, whether good or bad. What will yours be? Consider this during your journey of development. It might be a very sad, depressing, or even a disgusting one, but there will be a legacy. By going through this book and practicing these suggestions, combined with your heart-felt determination and commitment, you can recreate, maintain, and nurture a new positive legacy that will outlast you, which will be passed down through your descendants from generation to generation.

If you put as much effort into writing down the answers to these questions as you do in breathing, you'll have the motivation needed to succeed. This newly found legacy will become your roadmap to a new and happy lifestyle!

Note: Personality types are very important issues that need to be kept in the back of your mind while reading this book. When we are talking about personality types, we are talking about one's "CORE" personality traits, which are how you most often behave daily. Everyone runs through a range of personality types from passive to aggressive, depending on the situation. The main goal is to achieve an assertive core as a lifestyle.

The next issue I need to bring out is that people who have been hurt repeatedly throughout their life, live in their heads. They don't feel in their heads, they feel in their hearts. I imagine you have heard it said about someone that he is a *"deadhead or brain dead?"* Well, that's not too farfetched; we don't feel in our brains.

Our brain is for logic and for processing our thoughts. Our hearts are for feelings; we feel emotionally. Therefore, we need to find a balance between our logical minds and emotional hearts. Our hearts are to temper our minds. I tell some of my clients, they need to take their issues out of their heads and place them in their hearts where they have a conscience. The heart is where we find the difference between right and wrong, and good and evil.

Note – Throughout this book I will be giving insight into some of my experiences. I grew up a very angry young man. I truly believe it would have made a huge difference in the choices I made in my life if I had this information then. I know this information to be true because I use it daily and can see and feel the results being assertive brings. It is extremely empowering.

What exactly is Self-Empowerment? The dictionary states that the Self is "being independent; it is your complete makeup, your thoughts, behaviors, ideas, goals, desires, aspirations, feelings, and emotions, etc.!" Empowerment is to, "give official authority, to delegate legal power, to take total control of one's self." If you achieve Self-Empowerment, you are taking total control of your life! Self-Empowerment is giving yourself permission to take control over every aspect of your personal life.

You possess the freedom of choice to live your life as you desire. The facts are, we do not control anyone, not our children, spouses, siblings, parents, friends…we control no one. However, we do control ourselves and how people and situations *"affect us."* We control our decisions, thoughts, anger, and our own happiness.

To achieve true Self-Empowerment, there are tools, techniques, and concepts you need to learn and understand. Think about baking a cake. Do you not have to read the recipe, follow directions, and use proper ingredients and baking temperature, and perhaps ask questions to make sure it comes out correctly? Absolutely!

Working on your first car engine, did you not have to learn

techniques and concepts, and use the correct tools for the job? Did you not ask many, many questions? Achieving self-empowerment is no different. Everything discussed in this book are those tools, techniques, and concepts of achieving and maintaining Self-Empowerment.

Through Self-Empowerment, you gain happiness, contentment and self-confidence. You may also achieve a positive self-image, as well as stronger, more favorable relationships, and likely much more. These tools, techniques, and concepts eventually become a lifestyle that you will live with on a day-to-day basis for the rest of your life. You will influence your children in a positive way to insure their personal success in life. Although we do not control others we do influence greatly. Influence is far more effective than control.

When Jesus Christ died for our sins, he gave us the greatest gift of all, which was the freedom of choice. Through Self-Empowerment, we regain that gift of independence. Having the ability and right to choose is, Freedom!

Question: What goes through your mind when someone other than you, makes efforts to control your thoughts, your feelings, and every aspect of your existence? How does this control make you feel?

Note – During my childhood, I was never allowed to express my feelings or my displeasures. However, when I did, I was punished. *I was told I didn't have a right to express my feelings.* When I attempted to talk about my dreams, they were described as silly, or stupid, or I wasn't good or smart enough to achieve them. The result was that I hated my life and all the people in it. Is this the way you were raised? Is this the way you want your children to be raised? As a boy growing up, I often asked myself, why am I here? Why was I born?

One of the most important concepts for attaining Self-Empowerment is a concept that needs to be accepted and owned by the individual, and that is *USA* (Unconditional Self Acceptance.)

If you completely accept yourself totally and unconditionally, how would you feel inside? What kind of relationships would you have? What kind of example would you be for your children? What would your career be like? At what level would your self-esteem and self-worth be? What could you accomplish in your life? What kind of influence would you be to others? At what level would your integrity be? USA is another vitally important goal that needs to be placed on our agenda for a successful, healthy, and independent life.

Learning Process

Have you ever wondered why you do what you do, think what you think, and respond the way you do? Why do others feel empowered to reach their potential when you do not? Why are others successful in their relationships, careers and love, and you are not? Have you ever asked yourself, *"why me? Why does this always happen to me?"* I have asked myself these questions more times than I would like to remember.

Have you ever cursed at God and blamed Him for all of your troubles, hurts, and disappointments, etc.? Do you blame everyone else for your failures and unhappiness? Were you ever told you weren't good enough, smart enough, pretty enough, tall enough, thin enough, etc.?

These things have a powerful impact on a child, well into adulthood. As an adult, these same thoughts, feelings, emotions, and beliefs continue to burden us. It is a fact that we all live what we learn and respond to how we are treated. Personally, I learned to believe I was less than nothing, and that I was not good or smart enough. When I made a mistake I was asked, why I did that. I was called a dumb ass, and was occasionally told I was smarter than that, etc. The truth was, I didn't know, and eventually I didn't care. My common sense was blinded by fear, resentment, and anger.

I was confused, and I didn't know who to turn to, what to do, or where to go. I learned to trust no one, especially adults. Does this sound familiar to you?

Generally, all parents want the best and even *want* better for their children than they had. However, several problems enter into this *"want."* The first problem lies in the fact that children do not come with a set of instructions and parents are not always equipped with the necessary tools for good parenting, relationships skills, or effective communication. We carry on the beliefs and practices of our parents and of society, which are usually incorrect and some are even mythical.

Children are expected to learn the majority of these important, life-impacting tools somewhere other than at home. So, what they learn is usually from the streets and from their equally uninformed peers. This is referred to as the blind leading the blind. Again, please understand that, **we live what we learn,** which has a very powerful impact on how parents raise their children and how children develop emotionally. Most parents will pass on behaviors they have learned in their life, whether positive or negative, intentional or unintentional.

In school, we are taught math, but we are *not* taught how to problem solve. We are taught English, Spelling, and Grammar, but we are not taught how to effectively communicate with one another.

Children are allowed to watch the violence, sex, and inappropriate behavior on TV and in the movies with no explanation or guidance from parents. Then, when something happens, it's easier to ignore the real causality of the bad behavior and place all the blame on the children. What's wrong with this picture? Children are allowed to listen to music filled with the same violence, sex, and inappropriate language. That's like leaving the barn door ajar and when the horses get out, beat the horses. Simply put, children are expected to learn about sex, drinking, drugs, communication, problem solving, anger management, and relationship skills all on their own.

I keep a sign posted in my office that offends most parents. It says, *"Isn't it ironic that parents constantly complain about the bad behaviors of their children, but deny any responsibility for them?"* (author unknown) Is this not a true statement?

Do you think there is a possibility that parents, schools, and society in general do not know how to teach these crucial subjects, which would explain why they place little or no priority on them? What goes through your mind when you stop and think about this? It is acceptable if one does not know how to teach these things, but don't you think it is important that they recognize this and are willing to commit to making sure their children learn them?

For many years there has been a serious controversy as to whether TV, video games, music, etc., cause children to become violent. This is absolutely not true! These do not cause anyone to become violent. However, they most definitely have a tremendous influence on how children view and live their lives, and what they can do in that life. What causes an individual to become violent is not narrowed to one single factor. It is a culmination of many contributing factors to facilitate these types of behaviors. Until families and our society (including Hollywood) opens their eyes and hearts and are willing to accept their responsibility in the creation of the problem, we will continue to experience needless violence among our youth and young adults.

I know that everything in my life has had some level of influence on me, be it a movie, a piece of music, radio, magazine, book, TV, or something other people have said. It doesn't matter whether it is violence or happiness, everything will have some level of influence on each of us. These outside influences have made me stop and think about my beliefs, behaviors, actions and feelings, my relationships with my wife and kids, and other family members. Simply put, all these experiences have influenced my total existence in some way. I have made some monumental changes in my life due to certain influences.

Timing is the key. I was tired of living and acting in a way that I now view as emotionally injurious to others. At times, I was physically damaging as well, and even hurtful to myself. My struggle was that I knew down deep inside, I was a different kind of person...a person that cared about others, one who possessed the capacity of being kind and considerate. Due to the influence I was raised with, combined with resentment, anger, fear, and feeling that I was forbidden to live the way I felt, I lived in emotional chaos.

Deep down, I was living a life that was created for me by others based on their opinions of me, and I realized much later in life that this type of lifestyle was psychologically destructive to me. My sense of self, self-esteem, and self-worth eventually became non-existent, which caused me to be uncaring toward others. In my heart, I had no identity, and I began to isolate, emotionally and physically. It is very important that you look at your personal influences. These have a direct affect on you and your relationships, and only you can decide what kind of life you want to live from this point forward.

Question: Since TV, films, music, and video games are not the direct cause of violence, and we have freedom of speech, does this negate our personal responsibility to guide, educate, and protect our children and ourselves? If you believe it does, this means you are placing more importance on the right to be creative than the safety and lives of your children and families! I am not suggesting we ban anything; I am saying we need tougher regulations and laws to protect and educate our youth. And parents need to take a more active role in their children's lives, as well as their own.

It is equally important that parents and teachers, grandparents, and society in general need to take responsibility for their actions or lack thereof. These individuals need to take responsibility to be active in their child's life where they give guidance in every aspect of life and be very much aware of what their children are doing, who they hang around with, where they go, and what they listen to and watch. This is a parents' responsibility, and it takes very little time to accomplish this. The problem today is that parents say they are too busy, so they use computers, television and video games, etc. as a babysitter. It has been said that it takes a community to raise children; it does! It is the responsibility of parents to prepare their children for the next stage in life.

Note: WE TEACH PEOPLE HOW TO TREAT US!

Parents cannot give their children those things they do not possess themselves! As in relationships, you cannot give respect, love, understanding, and effective communication if you don't personally possess those characteristics or *tools*, can you? When a child gets in trouble, we do our best to blame the child, while ignoring the real causality of the event. In society, it is commonplace to focus on the person instead of the issue or event. This is not to say we should excuse the bad behavior. I am saying there are other factors that need to be considered to prevent this from reoccurring in the future. Bad behaviors can be changed in an effective and healthy way.

"*Understanding*" is an interesting concept. If you acquire a good understanding of any problem, then you'll dramatically improve your chances of fixing it; you don't necessarily have to fix every problem yourself. However, it is important you know where to get help when needed. Being open to getting help makes solutions easier to find. You'll experience less frustration and anger, thereby allowing you to confront issues with a logical and levelheaded demeanor. You'll be less judgmental and angry and you'll be more interested in fixing the problem or behavior, and not the person.

I believe it is true that parents want to give their children a better life than they had. Maybe then they might be willing to consider learning the appropriate tools and concepts themselves, so they enable their children with self-empowerment to live that better life. Remember the old saying, *"if we give a man a fish, he can eat for a day, but if we teach him HOW to fish, he can eat for a lifetime."* The same concept is true here.

Let's look at this process in a very simplistic way. When things are bogged down by psychobabble or politically correct dialogue, they become convoluted, frustrating, and extremely difficult to learn.

Paterson wrote the Assertiveness Workbook, and there is a concept in assertiveness training referred to as the **Bonsai Principle**. It means to keep it short, simple and to the point. I believe that when we go back to basics and keep things fundamentally simple, they are easier to understand, to utilize, and much easier to pass on to our children and others.

Note – For years, I lived what I learned, and I saw it was all negative. Because of that, I was angry with God and blamed Him for all of my misery. If I didn't blame Him, I blamed everyone else. I believe I was given the wrong information concerning God. However, I had feelings inside of me that told me there was a better way of life, and I knew I could have it, if only I could find the way. When I got older and began to understand these concepts, tools, and techniques, I found I had a decision to make. Do I want to stay living this way or change? I had to decide whether I wanted to be right or to be happy, and I knew *I was tired of being angry and bitter!* I decided life could not be any worse if I changed... it was either going to get better or stay the same.

I ultimately found the way, which has helped me overcome many hurdles in my life. I know I am a better person as a result and have also improved my marriage. In addition to this, I accepted God into my life and into my marriage, and I've stopped blaming Him. Instead, I thank Him daily for what I do have. I stopped blaming everyone else and have accepted personal responsibility for my life and for how I treat others. I am not always right, but I am happy 99% of the time. Therefore, I am a success because my success is measured by the quality of my relationships, and how I can touch others in a way that helps them do well for themselves. Let's begin our journey and examine how behavior is created.

Behavior

This is a brief explanation of how a child develops their core beliefs and behaviors, using Tommy as an example. Following this, we will segue into how and why people of all ages experience difficulties such as, addictions, unsuccessful relationships and careers, domestic violence, a lack of confidence, low or no self-esteem, and so on. I would like to emphasize that this explanation of behavioral development is very general in nature, but extremely powerful.

Learning is easier when the information is simplified to a level that's not insulting or offensive, and when people can apply the information to their personal lives and circumstances.

Simplistically, behaviors are created as shown below:

THOUGHTS   -->   FEELINGS   -->   EMOTIONS

(Beliefs)   *(Actions & Consequences)*

Everything begins with a thought; through time and repetition, it becomes a belief. These thoughts and beliefs will dictate our emotions and how we feel, and weigh heavily on the choices we make. Emotions are broken down into two categories, actions and consequences.

Note – Pay close attention as this is vitally important. As a child grows up, having been completely indoctrinated with parents distorted and sometimes ugly thoughts, these thoughts actually become solid personal beliefs within the child. Remember that our beliefs directly affect our feelings... Allow me to clarify.

When someone believes whole-heartedly that they are worthless, they actually begin to feel and act that way. They feel low, disgusted, embarrassed, hurt, and shallow. Because this child feels as though they are valueless and when someone sees some wonderful characteristic in them, and they relate it to the child, he or she will have extreme difficulty believing the compliment. In many cases, the child will never believe they are NOT worthless. To overcome these types of distorted beliefs, patience, love, and guidance must be abundantly available to them. Examine this to see if any of this sounds familiar?

Example: Tommy is having difficulty in school, carrying grades that do not meet the parent's or the teacher's expectations. If the parent loses patience with Tommy and out of frustration comments to him, *"you're stupid." "You can do this, stop being lazy."* The thought that is now in Tommy's mind is that he is stupid and lazy. If comments like these continue, what do you think Tommy will believe about himself? In almost every situation, he will begin to believe that he is stupid and lazy. This kind of negative propaganda is extremely harmful to the child in the long run. As this type of treatment continues, the frustration builds in the parent and the child, and at times the parent may strike out at the child. The child will begin to strike out as well; hence bad behaviors are created. Tommy may experience not only emotional abuse, but also physical abuse; thereby reinforcing the thought that he is stupid and lazy.

Tommy has now adopted a negative belief about himself from the people that are supposed to love and protect him. Even though parents have good intentions, they are unaware of the damage they are doing to the child. This negative belief dictates how he feels about himself, about school, and others. These feelings will also dictate how he treats himself and others. There is a definite chance that Tommy will begin traveling down a road of self-destruction.

Now let's examine his level of confidence, self-esteem, and his self-image. Do you think his desire to progress and attain a good education has been affected? Absolutely!

According to the behavior diagram on page 11, it shows that Tommy's thoughts, beliefs, and feelings will dictate how he is going to react emotionally. With this example, what do you think this child will eventually do? Do you think he might be headed for self-destruction, or rebellion such as substance abuse, legal problems, self-mutilation, etc?

Finally, what consequences do you believe he will experience due to these actions? Could it possibly be addiction, jail, prison, failed relationships, emotional suicide, death, or all the above? Keep in mind this story has been simplified for you to get a clearer understanding. The consequences that Tommy might go through are a direct result of the types of thoughts, beliefs, and feelings a parent, teacher, or society might have instilled in him.

The negative beliefs that Tommy or any child is raised with are referred to as cognitive distortions (thoughts), and by repetition, they become automatic thoughts. For instance, if a child is raised in a family that shows prejudice toward minorities, the child will adopt those same beliefs and will most likely be prejudiced as their parents. Therefore, when the child sees a minority, he/she will react according to that bigoted belief.

Automatic thoughts are those that continually resonate in your mind that cause you emotional and or relationship pain. They come to mind when you see, hear, or smell something familiar that triggers those beliefs. Thoughts and beliefs are created, not only by what a parent or guardian says and does, but equally by what they do not say or do. If this child is indoctrinated with de-structive comments like they are no good, or they are stupid and so on, these are those thoughts that continue to come to mind.

It is important to remember that we do not and cannot control our children or anyone else. However, we can and do influence them, and we need to take full responsibility for *how* we influence them. As parents, we have a responsibility to guide and prepare our children for adulthood, to be a productive member of society. Through the tools, techniques, and concepts we will discuss, you'll learn how to guide and influence others more effectively.

Generally, children develop their core beliefs between the ages of 5 and 12. Children are not born with hate, anger, violence, prejudice, addiction, or other forms of bad behavior. Children are born innocent, with a clean slate. As parents and society, we write upon that slate, so it is imperative we be careful of what we write. *Bad behaviors are learned!* As children grow older and begin entering the adult world of dating, the influences they have received from parents, friends, media, and so on, have a direct affect on their beliefs of how relationships should be. In other words, children are taught to either have disastrous or successful relationships!

Stop and think for a moment. Every personal interaction we engage in can be viewed as a level of a relationship. As in all relationships, it is important to understand that both parties have equal responsibility to affect positive results without contamination. Assertiveness is one of the most important tools we can use to create effective communication. We will examine communication in some depth later in the book. Keep in mind that approximately 95 percent of all communications are non-verbal; this communication is body language, facial expressions, and vocal intonations.

Let's look at the most important conceptual tool we have available to us today. It is attainable for every human being on the planet. It is also the most overlooked, misunderstood, and unused tool we have. The tool I'm referring to is assertiveness! I frequently ask people from varying occupations, what assertiveness means to them. Most often, I receive definitions believing it to be a form of aggression. That's not surprising, since we are a nation of aggressive and competitive people. Most everyone feels they are assertive. However, if you examine these individuals you'll find the greater majority are not.

ASSERTIVENESS

What is assertiveness, and what does it mean to be assertive? Assertiveness is *"A style or form of effective communication to achieve what we NEED!"* To achieve self-empowerment, it's important to be familiar with the components that characterize assertiveness. The following statistics give plenty of reasons why you would want to become assertive. Consider these very seriously. Are you or someone you know included somewhere in the following statistics?

During 2005, in the United States alone, it was estimated that every 9 seconds a woman was physically abused, which equates to 9,600 per day, or 292 thousand per month, and over 3.5 million per year. Four women are beaten to death every day. That amounts to more than 1400 women per annum. One of three women will experience some form of abuse! One out of nine women is raped, and over 50% of women will be involved in an extra marital affair! These are horrific statistics.

The process of assertiveness is not a do or die process. As you transition from where you are to be assertive, you will make mistakes and there will be times you'll slide back into old behaviors. It is important to remember that the longer you work at being assertive, the stronger and more proficient you will become. Understand that making mistakes is okay! You may offend people at times, and you may feel like giving up occasionally; I'm asking you not to…, Please do not quit! It is very important to remember that this tool, this concept of being assertive is NOT a strategy for getting what you want, or for getting your way. It is a communication style to be used for obtaining what you *"NEED!"* Recognize when you offend someone and have the good manners to acknowledge your error and apologize. This will do several things for you personally as you earn respect from others, which will boost your self-esteem and self-worth. You will develop credibility causing your confidence to increase; isn't this what you are attempting to attain?

WARNING: It has been my experience that when some people become proficient with assertiveness, they realize they can use it as a weapon to get back at those who have hurt them. It is easy to fall into this trap... and I caution you NOT to do it.

Again, assertiveness is a style or form of effective communication that will help you create, maintain, and nurture your relationships, self-esteem, and self-confidence. It will also enable you to set reciprocal boundaries in all your relationships. I am referring to all relationships, whether intimate, casual, familial, or professional.

In today's environment, both children and adults are under extreme pressure to fit in and be strong during a crisis. When an emergency arises, people become overwhelmed with frustration and stress, which can turn into anger. If they have never been taught the skills, tools, and techniques of problem solving, decision-making, and effective communication, these frustrations and stressors may run rampant. Often times' people may turn toward the use of anger, violence, drugs, alcohol, and/or sex to alleviate or minimize the feelings and stress they are experiencing. The end-result could be anything from domestic violence, addiction, jail, destroyed relationships, unemployment, and even death.

If you think back to the diagram of how behavior is created, can you see how this is applicable? I am sure you all have heard from time to time that there needs to be balance for you to have a relatively stress free life. While this is very true, we will look at the different types of balance in another chapter.

Note -- Growing up, I never knew of the concept of having your needs in balance, nor did I know how to achieve this balance. As an adult, this concept was intriguing to me. When I looked into it more, I learned that assertiveness is the key to acquiring the tools and techniques required to achieve that balance. This is what I am offering you in this book. Again, assertiveness is a form or style of effective communication to achieve what you need. It is a suit of armor, as it were, to protect us emotionally and sometimes physically. I like to refer to it as *"emotional body armor."*

As I began to apply ALL the concepts of assertiveness in my life, it started to change for the better. I began to feel important, not haughty or better than anyone else, but equal. I began to feel that I not only had a place in life, but I had a right to be there... just as you do. Isn't that what you want to feel and believe? I learned about my personal rights as a human being and I began to like and respect myself more every day. I concluded that I would let no one ever again hurt me, control me, or manipulate me. I had the choice with whom I would share my life as well as with whom I would not allow in my life. If I used these next two concepts properly, they would become another powerful tool that would be available to me; these are the concepts of individual decision and control. It is important for everyone to understand that our life requires balance in order to be healthy and meaningful.

"A true friend is someone who reaches
for your hand and touches your heart."
~Author Unknown~

CHAPTER 2

What Needs Afford You the Opportunity to Have a Balanced Life?

There are two required sets of needs that assist us in having a balanced life. One is environmental and the second is personal. Let's look at environmental first.

Environmental Needs

All of mankind has required needs. This set of needs is specifically for adults. Children have a similar set of needs, substituting career for school. They are as follows:

1. Physical Health
2. Mental Health
3. Career
4. Social Life
5. Private Time

Keep in mind that if one of these areas is negatively affected, the remaining needs will be impacted as well, creating an imbalance.

Let's look at each one of these, beginning with physical health. If your physical health is poor, this will cause your mental health to diminish and cause distractions in the other 'needs' areas. Your career and social life will likely suffer and your private time may come to a screeching halt. On the extreme side, your private time could translate to isolation and depression.

Private time is the need most often neglected. They rationalize and justify their reasons for not taking private time. They use silly excuses such as, *"I don't have time; I work too much." "My children and husband keep me so busy that I don't have any time for myself,"* etc. These are nothing more than excuses. This is not to belittle you or your reasoning; however, I will say that when you *need* something bad enough, you will almost always find a way to get it. Isn't this correct? Private time has to be a priority. This is the time you use to clear your head and heart of the ugly, nonsensical, and frustrating problems of the day. It's a time to relax and unwind emotionally and physically so you have an opportunity to regroup for the next go around. Private time is so important for you, your family, and all aspects of your life.

Your children also need this time. Their environmental needs are as important to them as yours are to you; however, theirs may need to be supervised.

Personal Needs

Let's switch our focus to personal needs, which are required for everyone. Specifically, and most importantly, they are mandatory for those adults raising children in an appropriate way to ensure a relatively happy and healthy life. Below are your personal needs:

1. Emotional
2. Physical
3. Social
4. Spiritual
5. Personal Security

If your personal needs are not in balance, then your ability to deal with everyday issues and your environmental needs will be hampered. Both groups of needs depend on each other for being fulfilled regularly and equally in order to create balance. Can this be done all the time… No! However, it is important to do your best, and if your emotional state is stressed, the rest of your needs will be shaken.

Notice that the spiritual category is on the list of environmental needs. Like adults, all children need a higher power to believe in, no matter what that may consist of. All of humanity *needs* something to believe in or turn to when life becomes overwhelming. I personally believe in God and Jesus Christ as my higher power. I go to Him with many inner secrets, feelings, and fears that no one else can help me with; this is called faith. People innately have to believe in or have faith in something that gives them strength, courage, guidance, and hope. Through this concept of higher-power, people can have a more fulfilling existence. This is so important for children growing up, and holds equal importance for adults. When my wife and I began to agree on our higher power and who He is, we both noticed less stress and frustration in our individual lives and in our relationship with one another. Faith in God offers unity in belief. It offers guidance in learning how to have faith, how to give and receive love, and how to forgive and care about other important things rather than ourselves. Faith can also unite the family or the relationship and create a common goal for strength. However, as with everything else this is your choice.

In all relationships, whether casual, intimate, familial, or professional, we have a responsibility to fulfill the needs of others to the best of our ability. This does not mean we have to cater to anyone, it means we have a responsibility to be cognizant, to be aware of their feelings and respect their reality. Respecting one's reality is simply to follow the golden rule and do not ignore the concept of respect. You might wonder why I use the term, concept so much. Until a particular concept is used and practiced, it is only a concept. When a concept is used and practiced, it becomes a tool, and when used every day, it becomes a lifestyle.

SUBCATEGORIES OF PERSONAL NEEDS

Parents, as well as children, need balance in their lives. In order for a child to have a relatively balanced life, it is important for parents to supply those needs for this to take place. Here's an example of how this works. Under physical **needs,** a few of the subcategories are physical interaction, acceptance, and structure. If a child does not have physical interaction with other children, then how can this child feel accepted by his peers? How will he/she learn to respect others or learn to communicate? If he/she doesn't have a structure, how will he/she feel accepted by parents and others in authority? What kind of existence will he/she have without proper structure in his/her life? Remember that when any subcategory of needs is negatively affected, all other categories and subcategories will be negatively affected and will result in a dysfunctional imbalance in our life. Following are the required subcategories of personal needs:

Physical:
1. Physical Interaction
2. Acceptance
3. Structure

Emotional:
1. Acceptance
2. Support
3. Validation

Social:
1. Social Interaction
2. Friends
3. Acceptance

Spiritual:
1. Higher Power
2. Acceptance
3. Faith

Personal Security:
1. Safe Environment
2. Parental Guidance
3. Acceptance

Let's examine the category of personal security and eliminate or drastically reduce the subcategory of safe environment. Applying all we have discussed so far, what do you think will happen? What other needs are affected if a safe environment is missing?

If a child does not feel safe in his/her own home, do you believe this child will have positive parental guidance or acceptance? Ask yourself about the other categories and subcategories; do you think any of those will be affected? If your answer is yes… you are correct; it has a domino effect. When one is affected, all are affected. This is why it is imperative that children's needs be met, for if they are not, behavioral problems will occur.

Think of how behaviors are created and review the diagram on page 11. This is how behavior is created. Can you see how this concept works?

The same occurs in all relationships. I have been asked many times about how difficult it is to fulfill one's needs. It really isn't hard if you practice true assertiveness, are aware of the needs and feelings of others, and take responsibility for how you influence them.

If you think back in time at some of the abusive moments you have experienced, and think about what we have discussed about needs and balance, you will see where many of your needs have been out of balance, completely removed, or neglected.

BEHAVIORAL CONCEPTS

What is it that we as individuals can control? There are only *three things* we have the ability to control. 1) We can control ourselves; 2) We can also control how people affect us, and 3) We can control how situations affect us.

You cannot control your children. You cannot control your spouse or other family members. You cannot control your employees or your best friends. Even so, there are those who will do their best to try to control whoever and whatever they can. Paterson broke these down in his book, the Assertiveness Workbook.

This is easier to understand when examining the five personality types:

1. Passive
2. Passive Aggressive
3. Aggressive
4. Assertive
5. Alternator

Note that these personality types do not represent people, they are all *"Learned Behaviors."*

Which type do you think you are? Write down what type you believe yourself to be. Be open and honest with yourself. Do not rationalize and justify one over the other just because you want to fit into a particular type. The majority of people fall into one of two types; they are either passive or passive-aggressive. A few people fall into the aggressive type and are easily spotted. The assertive type is also very few in number, but readily detected. The alternator type is easily spotted as well, but thankfully few in numbers. The passive and passive-aggressive types are more difficult to identify. Keep in mind that all of us will experience 4 out of 5 of these types daily. It is the *"core"* personality type we are referring to here, the type that represents our personality regularly.

Personality Types

PASSIVE PERSONALITY

The passive personality type is often referred to as a 'doormat' because these individuals will do anything and everything to please others. This person is commonly found in households with a dominating and abusive parent or spouse.

These dominating persons use tactics such as demeaning language, fear, manipulation, bribery, threats, violence, guilt or shame to control and manipulate their victim. The passive person possesses little or no life skills, relationship skills, effective communication skills, no self-esteem, and no self-confidence. They have a severe lack of self-respect and self-worth. They are fearful when it comes to defending themselves; therefore, they don't. Their lives may become hopeless and isolated. They prefer to be a fly on the wall. They have no identity, no individuality, and they become isolative and fearful of others and of their own beliefs. They often slouch and will avoid making eye contact.

Passives apologize for everything. They keep quiet. They never talk about their feelings, emotions, or needs. They refuse to argue their point, and they fear rejection. When it comes to confrontation, they feel helpless. They become frustrated and confused, and they will almost always turn their control over to the aggressor.

PASSIVE AGGRESSIVE PERSONALITY

This person is described as one who mimics the passive type. When they fail to meet the expectations of others, they fall into a denial mode. They use excuses as their defense. They conveniently forget and they always have an excuse. Passive aggressive types reject responsibility and accountability. This type of person believes they are entitled to be in total control, even after making commitments to others. They do not take responsibility for their own actions and believe they will be rejected if they are more assertive.

This person becomes resentful of the demands and requests of others. They fear confrontation. They do whatever it takes to get their way without taking responsibility or being noticed. They prefer to stay in the background. They will pit one person against another. They are instigators. They use excuses or point fingers and place blame to remove the focus from themselves.

AGGRESSIVE PERSONALITY

The aggressive person makes himself or herself larger than life to threaten and intimidate others. This personality makes fixed and penetrating eye contact. Their voices are loud, even on the verge of shouting. However, if the yelling does not work they will lower their voice in hopes of intimidating their victims. They feel their needs and desires to be much more important and justified than those of others. They are better, superior, and more valuable than anyone else. Their emotions are filled with anger and power, and they have to win at all cost. They absolutely hate to lose.

Sometimes they feel guilt and remorse afterward and will ask for forgiveness. They swear they will never do it again… but they do. They do it again, and again, even to a violent end.

This aggressive type of person feels a need to control the people around them all the time. They ultimately belittle, ignore, reject, and insult the needs, desires, dreams, and wants of others around them. They become physically and emotionally violent and/or abusive. This type of person can be very dangerous. They seldom succeed in intimate or professional relationships.

ALTERNATOR PERSONALITY

The main problem with this individual is that they swing from extreme passiveness to extreme aggressiveness with little or nothing in between; this is done in the blink of an eye. They experience a major melt down to the point of violence and then go back to a passive mode until they are angered again. These people are ticking time bombs; stay clear of this personality.

They possess little or no conscience.

ASSERTIVE PERSONALITY

The Assertive personality type is the most desirable to achieve, as well as the most difficult. Changing life-long behavior is the most arduous thing to accomplish because it entails changing your physical and emotional life patterns, specifically your thoughts and beliefs. It is making a commitment to yourself to accept full responsibility and accountability for your own actions, thoughts, beliefs, and behaviors for everything that takes place in your life! Again, this is not an easy task. However, the results are extremely rewarding.

If you commit to this change, you will develop a more positive outlook on life. Instead of looking at the downside of life, your problem solving skills will increase, and you will be capable and more interested in looking at other possible solutions.

The body movements of an assertive person are relaxed, confident, and laid-back. Assertive people deliver regular eye contact when speaking with someone. They feel positive about themselves and treat others in kind. Their self-esteem, self-confidence, and sense of self are sharpened and more defined. Their self-respect is improved as is their respect for others. In the relationships they develop, there are no controlling issues or tactics involved.

They respect the reality of others. Respecting one's reality does not mean you have to agree with it, like it, or even accept it. It means that you respect that person's right to their opinion and their reality. The assertive person accepts their right to express their needs, feelings and emotions, openly and honestly. They don't project unfair expectations onto others. They allow others to own their personal points of view and to possess their own beliefs. Assertive people place value on these characteristics for others and for themselves. They do not judge or belittle others. The needs of others have equal standing to their own. After reading this description, you might feel it impossible to achieve this personality type; it really isn't.

It is the most calming and comforting lifestyle I have encountered. I find the relationships I desire most have improved and strengthened. I respect myself more and find that I draw respect from others without much effort. Stress and frustration are reduced. Let me clarify that this is not utopia nor is it a fantasy lifestyle; being assertive means taking control of your life and your person. Clients I have worked with who practice these tools and techniques are more secure and independent and tend to live happier lives.

Keep in mind that these behavioral types are just that. ALL behaviors are learned and we live what we learn! We can all relearn good behaviors and throw out the bad.

How were your behaviors and beliefs learned? What behavior type are you? Do you feel a need to make changes in your life for yourself and your family?

Keep in mind that all behaviors begin with a thought. For every negative, hurtful comment (verbal abuse) we give to another person, it takes 1000 positives or helpful comments to remove it. What does this show you about the harsh impact of verbal abuse? It is my opinion that verbal and emotional abuse is more severe than physical abuse. These two forms of abuse are addressed much less often than are other forms of abuse and sustain longer lasting, negative effects.

By becoming assertive, you learn to thwart those types of negative behaviors, and you influence others to follow suit. When you do, you'll begin to see those who have previously taken advantage of you, abused you, or lied to you will stay away from you because they are fearful of your new-found confidence.

Question: What is a true gift?

A true gift is something you give from the heart with no expectation of return. This is a gift you not only give yourself, but to others. Assertiveness is the *MOST* effective and the *LEAST*

OFFENSIVE form of all the communication styles we possess. When you begin to practice assertiveness, your life perceptions begin to change as well.

It is very *IMPORTANT* to remember that when developing an assertive lifestyle, people who know you will likely get upset with you because they don't understand what you are doing. The behaviors you were known to previously possess will begin to change. Most people do not like to experience change, especially if there is a chance of losing control over that person, and some may get upset or even angry with you. Do not be surprised if this happens and do not allow this to cause you to give up. If a friend gets upset or angry with you for trying to improve yourself, ask yourself if they were truly your friend in the first place. If it is a family member that gets upset with you, do they really have a meaningful place in your life, or do they want to control you?

For example, if you are a passive personality type, and you become assertive, there are people that might conclude that you are angry. They see your submissive behavior leaving, and they watch while you take control of your life. This may annoy people to the point of anger in some cases. You need to be aware of this so that you don't allow others to force you back into your old passive behavior. The best way for someone to assist you with this change is for you to explain what you are doing and ask for help from those you trust. Ask your friends to let you know when you become passive, passive-aggressive, or aggressive. This will also accomplish something else. Those who want only to control you will begin to filter away. Don't be alarmed because this is what you want to happen! Remember, the fewer people attempting to control you, the better chance you have of becoming assertive and living the life you want.

Let's do a quick self-assessment. Be honest with yourself as you answer these questions.

Know that all behaviors can be changed if you have a desire to learn the tools, concepts, and techniques and have the will to

commit yourself to that change. The rewards of change far out-
weigh the costs. Write your answers down for future review.

1. What personality type do you fit?
2. What causes you to become aggressive?
3. Do you have difficulty being assertive?
4. What is your biggest fear in becoming assertive?
5. What 2 people do you find it most difficult to be assertive
   with?
6. When are you most likely to get assertive?
7. If your core personality type is passive, what causes you to
   turn your aggression inward?

I find it helps to ask yourself this question, especially when you
find yourself in difficult times of decision-making. "Do I want to be
RIGHT or do I want to be HAPPY?"

This question really does help. Life is wonderful as it is nothing more than an *"Individual Choice,"* no matter what it is we are
deciding. Even if it's dealing with a terminal disease, we have a
choice to either fight the disease with everything we have or sit
back and allow it to consume us! Think about that for a moment!
If you're a Christian, remember that Jesus died not only to free
us from our sins, but to give us a *"choice."* Do not allow anyone
to take your right to choose away from you!!!! Do not give your
rights away either.

"Understanding is the key to our existence."

~Lee Braddock~

CHAPTER **3**

What Prevents You From Becoming Assertive?

What prevents you from being Assertive? How are you suffering by not being assertive?

These are the main stumbling blocks that interfere with you becoming assertive.

1. Stress
2. Fear
3. Dysfunctional Beliefs (Cognitive Distortions)
4. Social
5. Gender

Stress

What is stress? What are the effects of stress on you? Stress is how your body reacts to change or how you perceive the un-expected that requires you to adjust to uncomfortable situations. It's important to understand that stress can be controlled to a great degree if you choose. Stress is not always a bad thing, it is a healthy thing if we do not allow it control our lives.

Stress is caused by everyday situations that arise; anything that forces you to make unexpected or unwanted changes in your life or environment. Our mind and body will react to these changes with a physical, mental, and emotional response. Everyone deals with these changes in their own way as stress affects people differently and at different levels.

Common Causes of Stress:	
Death of a loved one	Traffic
Divorce	Marriage
Pregnancy	Legal problems
New job	Retirement
Health problems	Children
Moving to a new location	Unwanted Confrontations
Loss of Job	Serious Accident
Financial Problems	Natural Disaster

Any major interference to your normal lifestyle will cause a certain degree of stress. Stress can reveal itself in many ways, such as headaches, upset stomach, and nervous disorders. Your body is a wonderfully unique system that lets you know when something isn't working correctly. It can do this in several ways. Your physical and emotional behavior will offer warning signs of stress.

Some of the physical signs you may experience are a slouched or poor posture, sweaty palms, headache, chronic fatigue, restlessness, irritability, alterations in your eating habits or weight, decrease in sexual activity, or physical or emotional isolation.

Some of the emotional signs of stress are anger, worry, sadness, mood swings, inability to concentrate, or disruption in your thought processes. **Stress affects your behavior, as well.** Signs to be aware of are increased alcohol or drug use, increased relationship problems, over-reacting to things that would not normally upset you, interruptions in sleep patterns, etc.

Here are a few suggestions for controlling stress, if you choose… Effectively communicate with someone you trust, ask for advice, and exercise (this is a big one). Reduce your expectations of others and accept that you can only control yourself and how situations affect you. Accept responsibility and accountability for *"your"* own actions. Learn effective problem solving skills and communicate your displeasures to the person(s) involved. Communicate your feelings, and emotions. Instead of relying on aggression or passive behavior, *LEARN TO BE ASSERTIVE*. Find, maintain, and nurture emotionally supportive relationships. Confront your cognitive distortions/thought distortions, (these will be discussed in the next section). Become self-aware; learn how and/or what caused the stress in the first place and make changes as needed. Learn to set reciprocal-boundaries to protect yourself, even if circumstances dictate that you separate yourself from a person, place, or thing that causes you stress. This may mean keeping your distance from a family member, a child *(if not a minor)*, co-worker, or a parent. Learn relaxation techniques to maintain and nurture your personal and environmental needs for a more balanced and healthy life.

Dealing with stress and other life experiences takes effort, desire, and most of all, commitment. The more coping strategies you learn and utilize, the more equipped you'll be to reduce and extinguish those stressful moments in your life. It is a process.

Much like fear, stress is caused by the unknown and things we are not sure how to manage. Very often, stress is caused by family members, work, traffic, and/or finances, specifically those people and events in our current environment.

Stress is the leading cause of heart attacks and strokes. It is also the leading cause of anger and domestic violence! I mention anger and domestic violence because these are two of the most important issues we are faced with today. Domestic violence is rising at an alarming rate with horrifying results on our children. Alcohol and drugs are strong contributors; stress is the number one contributor to death!

In this book, you will see how assertiveness will have a positive effect on negative behaviors. Assertiveness can help problem solving and decision-making skills necessary to reduce stress, anger, and incidence of domestic violence.

Note: Anger is similar to alcohol and drugs; anger is controlling. It engulfs our entire being and takes over our thoughts, decision-making processes and common sense. It changes our personality to something unacceptable and toxic to both others and ourselves. It is destructive and changes our existence, just as with alcohol and drugs.

Because alcohol, drugs, and addiction play a serious part in many relationships, it is important to mention that even addiction is a learned behavior. It is a destroyer of relationships and careers. Many people who read that addiction is a learned behavior may be upset, angry or even confused. I ask only that you have an open mind and heart to consider another point of view. Believing that all behaviors are learned is as important to your success as breathing is essential to living.

When confronted with a stressful situation, ask yourself, *"what is it that I can control in this situation?"* Since nine times out of ten, the answer is going to be nothing, why do you want to waste your time, energy, and emotional health, or risk your personal safety?

When you are not sure of the exact cause of your stress, it helps to know the warning signs. Once you identify these signs, you have learned how your body responds to stress, and you can take steps to reduce it; this is self-awareness! When your stress turns into fear, the bodily response can do one of three things; you will fight, flight, or freeze.

FEAR

I want to clarify that this section on fear is related to the generalized concept of natural fear, not phobic disorders. What is fear?

Fear is simply a bodily response to one's perception of a threat. This threat can be a physical and/or a psychological threat. Fear is also a form of insecurity. Insecurity is a feeling that begins in childhood and is carried through our adulthood.

Think about this, *"what you fear, you will create!!"* What this concept is saying is, if you have a specific fear, and you think about it long enough, you will eventually create that fear in your own mind, which can manifest itself in any situation. It is no different than creating what we believe. Fear is a very interesting and common phenomenon. It is one of the most powerful emotions we possess. In many cases, I believe it can be more influential than love. If we have a clear understanding of what fear is and why we experience it, we will realize it is nothing more than a warning device that can protect us from harm.

Fear and confusion are very controlling tools and easily causes us to be negatively influenced. Selfish, uncaring, violent, and devious persons use fear to control or manipulate and may use it as a weapon against others and ourselves. These individuals use fear to confuse, take advantage and generally hurt others. We have all known people who have used fear in this manner.

Remember, emotions are broken down into two categories… actions and consequences. Now let us tie our needs into the equation. One of the most important needs every human being requires is acceptance. Of course, the lack of acceptance is viewed as rejection. Most people are fearful of rejection, change, confrontation, feelings of inadequacy, worthlessness, hopelessness, death, unemployment, and criticism, just to name a few.

A large majority of men will deny they are fearful of anything; this is consistent with how men are raised. However, if you deprive one of these men of their required needs, they will eventually become fearful, then angry, and possibly violent. Fear is one of the main ingredients that lead to anger. Anyone who denies they experience fear is either a liar or a fool. Fear is a great controlling tool, as many victims of domestic violence will attest.

The concept of fear is often misunderstood. We use fear for entertainment to frighten someone for fun, or to get a laugh. We get excited to watch a horror movie during the Halloween season. On the other hand, we ignore and react to real fear in an unhealthy way. If we allow ourselves to gain an understanding of fear, what causes it and how it works, then wouldn't we be more apt to deal with it in a more logical and healthy manner?

Keep in mind that during a fearful experience, the hippocampus area of the brain is set off and the experience is automatically stored in our memory banks or subconscious mind. Then sometime later when you experience something by sight, smell, or hearing that is related to a specific event that caused you to feel threatened in the first place, your bodies will instantly react in the same way.

We were all created with built in senses and one of these senses allows us to perceive danger, threats, or anything in our environment that may cause us harm. These are called instincts, and I suggest that everyone learn to decipher, understand, and listen to them. This is simply another of the built in protections we all possess.

Our brain is probably the most powerful and effective computer in existence. The brain will automatically store every experience we have, regardless of the severity. These experiences can be extreme happiness, sadness, hurtful, or traumatic events.

One amazing thing about the brain is its ability to cross-reference. This system assists us with instant recall of our experiences. Regardless of how insignificant or traumatic the experience, the memories are automatically stored in our subconscious. It is important to remember that whether we remember the exact experience or not, it doesn't matter. When the cross-reference system kicks in and detects a negative experience, we will most likely experience fear again or at the very least, we will have some emotional discomfort.

Consider your life experiences. These experiences dictate how you perceive the individual events of your life. Negative life experiences should never be allowed to control you. They should be viewed as tools for guidance or lessons that need to be learned. They should also be used to develop reciprocal boundaries, which are used for personal protection. If negative life experiences become your main focal point, you will become fixated on fear and anger with little ability to move forward.

Fear stifles your thought processes, problem solving, and decision-making abilities. It inhibits your ability to trust, respect, love, or commit to anyone or anything. If it is not understood and dealt with appropriately, fear is a debilitating emotion. We ultimately pass our fears, behaviors, and beliefs down to our children! This is one way children develop cognitive distortions.

HOW DOES FEAR PROGRESS?

Think back to the behavioral diagram while reading this section and consider the following steps:

ONE: Fear begins with a thought. If you think someone you care about does not like you, respect you, or is angry with you, feelings of fear will begin. You may be negatively criticized if you feel inadequate, worthless, or hopeless, which may create fear in you, as well. Again, your brain is wonderfully complex. At the sign of any of these triggers, your body goes into action, preparing to deal with that perceived threat.

TWO: When confronted with stress that turns into fear, the bodily response will likely be to fight, flight or freeze. FIGHT: You'll fight as hard as you can to *REDUCE* the threat. There is only one reason to ever lift a hand toward another person and that is in the physical defense of yourself or another person. FLIGHT: You'll run as hard as you can to *ESCAPE* the threat. Keep in mind, especially in domestic situations involving a child's safety, children will run and emotionally isolate. This is the only form of protection they know. Adults also isolate emotionally when they feel they have no other option. The problem occurs when people realize they do have a choice, and fear stops them from making that choice.

If you think about the concepts of fight and flight, what does this tell you about your life? If you are living in a physically and/ or emotionally abusive relationship, please take these concepts to heart and get out. You should not stand toe to toe and fight.

You have a responsibility to protect yourself and your children by means other than physically fighting.

FREEZE: This one is seldom reviewed. Alternatively, you may become so *FRIGHTENED* that you physically freeze. The fear you are experiencing is so intense you cannot move your body, your muscles freeze, and you are unable to think and feel.

Because of that intense fear, you may instinctively avoid any direct or indirect contact with the cause of that fear. You may say things, do things, or make choices that you normally would not. These things have a way of coming back to haunt you.

THREE: If things don't work out as hoped, your negative feelings, thoughts, and beliefs about yourself will be qualified, quantified, and supported, and many times intensified. This will cause you to become more fearful and may increase doubt about your own abilities, thereby lowering your self-esteem, confidence, and sense of self. You might feel as though you have *"failed."* You will begin to dislike and disrespect yourself, and you may settle for less in life than you deserve. This may include choosing to enter into unhealthy and unsafe relationships, causing further destruction.

FOUR: You finally come to the end of your rope, and begin to search for some method of numbing your emotional pain. Life becomes more confusing and frustrating. You find that the usage of alcohol or drugs, unsafe sexual contact, cutting yourself, overeating, bad relationships or emotional or physical isolation might reduce the pain. The reality of this is that it only *"Worsens"* your problems. These methods begin to deteriorate your mind, body, and relationships. You begin to make choices concerning your life according to those negative thoughts and beliefs *"others"* have put into your mind and have taught you to believe about yourself.

Question: What is the most important aspect of self-destructive behaviors that should be seriously examined? Do you think it might be prudent to truthfully consider the causality of each of these behaviors? It is the desire of this author that readers identify the causality of the self-destructive behaviors, because you cannot fix what you do not identify and acknowledge.

Changing any behavior or attitude begins with an understanding and awareness of how these affect you. Here are a few suggestions:

If you become aware and have an understanding of your fears and how they affect you, then you can become proactive in the solutions for your life.

Review the facts! Do not be concerned about what you may think or perceive. Begin narrowing down your fears to one specific fear. When you've done this, you will then be able to analyze it, understand it, and ultimately find a solution.

Please understand that *FEAR KILLS*! It will kill your desires; it will kill your dreams, your careers, your relationships, and eventually your spirit.

How Does Fear affect you?

Some of the effects can be measured as shown in the table below:

INCREASES	DECREASES
Emotions	Creative thinking
Heart rate	Ability to Problem Solve
Pulse	Ability to Manage your Anger
Respiration	Ability to Communicate properly
Blood Sugar	Ability to Focus
Blood supply to Muscles	Ability to Feel
Release of Endorphins (natural pain killers)	
Risk of Stroke or Heart Attack	

Again, you can reduce your fear and stress. Consider developing an exercise program, creating a good nutritional dietary schedule, reducing your caffeine intake and reviewing the personal and environmental needs list that leads to a balanced life. It is very important to reduce those associations that cause you stress. Many times domestic violence is the main cause of the majority of stress and fear in a family unit, and these are the most destructive individually. Regardless of its bad taste, this is one of my favorite sayings because it carries a lot of meaning; *"If you don't want any do-do on you, don't hang with it."* In other words, make a choice not to be around people that want to control and hurt you!

Note: When two people fight, they generally fight about a topic NOT related to the real issue. However, if you or a partner focus on the real issue in an argument, the hostility would most likely be lessened. By focusing on the *"real"* issue, do you think a discussion could begin that may result in a positive outcome? Do you think it could reduce the possibility of domestic violence?

Let's briefly look at how domestic violence engulfs every member of the family. When parents argue and fight, they lose focus on the welfare and needs of their children and each other. Therefore, the children begin to feel rejected because the parents want *"to win no matter what."* Often, the children begin to wonder what he or she has done wrong to create the hostile environment. Because the child's needs are being thwarted, his or her existence has turned upside down. Their self-esteem, self-respect, and confidence are eventually diminished or destroyed. The feelings of guilt and shame also enter this scenario. Children have a unique way of rationalizing and justifying why they are responsible for the problems of their parents.

As fear sets in, feelings of rejection become their emotional reality, which grows to the point of self-blame and progresses into anger. They ultimately develop a self-destructive behavior and may rebel and seek out acceptance from other sources, such as from gangs, sex, alcohol, or drugs. Their trust in authority has been damaged, as well. Parents are usually completely unaware of what their actions are doing to the child, and are oblivious to their own responsibility about the child's behavior.

I keep a sign in my office that says, *"Isn't it ironic that parents constantly complain about their child's bad behavior and attitudes, but refuse to accept any responsibility for them?"* In many cases, parents become so involved with their own issues they forget about their child, and it appears as if they don't care.

Parents and society focus on what the child has done wrong or is doing wrong, when they should be focusing on the *causality* of the child's bad behavior. The consequences can be devastating to the child and the family unit. Parents, society, schools, and businesses all need to become *"proactive"* when it comes to dealing with all bad behaviors, regardless of age.

Let's take this one step further. When this boy/girl grows into young adulthood, they will carry these feelings, beliefs, and behaviors with them. Think about your situation. Then, most generally they fall into bad relationships that continue to support those feelings and beliefs. The true reality of it is that their self-esteem, self-image, and self-respect continue to deteriorate and as a result, their self-destructive behavior worsens.

They get involved in unsuccessful and volatile relationships, while their happiness and success become nothing more than a passing dream. What kind of future does this child have to look forward to? How will these individuals be treated by family members and society when they are simply living what they have learned? All of us have an equal responsibility toward people, regardless of age or relationship, to ensure that those individuals have their needs met. From childhood, we are taught fear in many forms; it's usually negative. With the proper tools, it can be used as a positive motivator to strengthen. If you examine the causality of your fear and are able to come to a clear understanding of the effects, your fear will be more manageable and you may possibly overcome it.

Many children are taught that they need to live up to other people's expectation, specifically parents and teachers. They are also taught that if they happen to be assertive, they are going to open themselves up to harsh criticism or personal attack. So they refrain from asserting themselves. Within the realm of fear and through their cognitive distortions, they tell themselves they have no right to voice their thoughts, ideas, or opinions. Eventually their fear grows and they become passive, which carries through into adulthood. Does this sound somewhat familiar?

Fear prevents us from doing what we need to do, or what we would like to do. We become fearful based on the perceptions of others as well as through our own life experiences and lack of knowledge. If the life experiences we have learned have been primarily negative in nature, the fear will be enhanced and distorted.

We have all heard the old saying, **"there is nothing to fear but fear itself."** That is a true statement. Wouldn't it be powerful if you could find the tools to support that statement? Study and learn the information in this book, and you will be on your way. It is simply gaining a clear understanding of what is causing us fear, which are those beliefs others have implanted in our heads. If we learn how to process the *facts* and not our *perceptions*, then fear would be reduced and become more manageable. Stress and our core beliefs are closely related in the concept of fear. Confrontation and criticism will be discussed at length in a later chapter.

I have talked a great deal about fear, and I have restated a few issues to make a point. As I stated earlier, fear is one of the most negatively influencing and controlling emotions we have.

Note: As I was growing up, fear of my stepfather, in combination with my hatred for him turned into anger and numbness. I reached a point in my life where I believed there was nothing more he could do to hurt me. I wasn't afraid of death. I felt I had suffered through so much by that time that I felt I wanted to die. All the concepts you have read about thus far are all components of behavior. As a parent or future parent, you are highly advised to consider everything in this book and put it into practice to be a positive influence on everyone in your world, especially to your children and yourself.

Automatic Thoughts (Core Beliefs) ━━━━━━━━━━━━━━

What are cognitive distortions or automatic thoughts? How do they affect you? Can you have automatic thoughts that are positive? Yes, absolutely! However, we need to examine the negative.

The thoughts we have as adults are originally learned from an early age. As children, we are indoctrinated with our parent's ideologies, beliefs, world views, prejudices, values, and morals, etc. The majority of our beliefs were taught by our parents, peers, through television, radio, music, and even through our own experiences. Please understand my intent is *NOT* to parent bash.

Note: Most children and adults learn by what they *SEE* rather than by what they hear! I do not believe in pointing fingers or placing blame because it is a characteristic that creates stress and contaminates and destroys relationships. The act of placing blame keeps us from accepting responsibility. The act of placing blame and pointing fingers thwarts communication, problem-solving skills, the decision-making process, and much more. Avoid pointing fingers or placing blame at all cost!

The next important concept is perception. Our behaviors, beliefs, feelings, and emotions are directly affected by our *"perceptions"* of a topic, rather than by the subject itself. Cognitive Behavioral Therapy is just one of the therapeutic modalities I use in my practice. Cognitive Behaviorists believe people do not react to what is really going on...rather, that people react to what they **perceive**. Therefore, when people argue or fight, they do so about superficial things rather than what is really going on around them. They simply don't know how to get to the real meat of the fight or argument. When all hell breaks loose, they find themselves in complete chaos.

If you are experiencing negativity in your life and relationships, keep in mind that many of our core beliefs or automatic thoughts are cognitive distortions or distorted thoughts. In many instances, these distorted thoughts may be misperceptions of what is real. Example: We all know that being prejudiced is wrong. It is equally as wrong to hate another human being for their color, religion, sexuality, or ethnicity, etc. However, if we were taught to believe this way, then our thoughts would be considered a cognitive distortion or distorted thought. I have found most people don't realize their distortions because they have never sat down and analyzed them. These distorted beliefs cause us to act in a non-assertive manner. They are not recognizable as distortions because they seem normal; it is what they were raised with. Rarely are we allowed to choose what we want to believe in our formative years.

Unfair Expectations

This concept has been one of the main causes for anger and resentment. This also has caused the destruction of many, many relationships. It is a troublesome, confusing concept that deserves and needs to be examined because everyone has them. Unfair expectations are created without any thought or consideration. According to the dictionary, *an expectation is the act of expecting; the act of anticipating.* It is referred to as a mental attitude that is often related to anticipating a positive outcome or a profit gain. Expectations are centered around *"us."* They pertain only to us; no one else. An expectation usually revolves around an anticipated positive conclusion that will benefit us physically, financially, mentally, or emotionally. Is it wrong to have expectations? That is a complicated question, nonetheless, a good one. It is not wrong if used correctly and fairly. The problem exists when it is used incorrectly and selfishly, hence *unfair expectations*.

What are unfair expectations? We have discussed what expectations are, so what makes them unfair? Unfair expectations are an *"entitlement,"* and a *"lack of communication."* These two concepts go hand-in-hand. This behavior is projected on to the people we love, people we work with, or those who work for us, family members, friends, and neighbors, as well as the general public.

Entitlement

"Entitlement" is that belief you have that it is your right, your privilege, your power, or your prerogative, and you demand your claim to it. I see people do this every day, and I hear it in their voices. As a respectful and courteous driver, have you ever been driving down the street and suddenly are cut off by another driver, which startles you? You get upset and yell at this person, calling them names and using vulgar language. Did you get angry because he cut you off or because you expect others to be as respectful and courteous as you are?

I have heard people say, *"I don't treat people that way and..."* This anger is caused by unfair expectations of others. My wife and I both have caught ourselves getting frustrated or being disappointed when people display a lack of the simplest common courtesies. For instance, have you ever been in a restaurant and suddenly you hear vulgar language erupt from a table near you while your children are near? How does that make you feel? What do you think your children are getting from this? Personally, I feel offended and angered because of their lack of consideration for my family and myself. If nothing is said, the children get the idea that this kind of behavior is acceptable. I certainly wouldn't use that kind of language in a public place, and I expect others would have the same kind of respect. The expectation that others be as respectful as you are is what gets most people upset, sometimes more than the language. Is this an unfair expectation? When looking at it socially, yes it is, because society has become immune to such rudeness and disrespect. Remember we teach people how to treat us. By not saying anything we are saying that bad, disrespectful behavior is okay. Looking at it from a personal perspective, no, it is not an unfair expectation, especially if something has been communicated.

When working with my clients, one of the major sources of their anger stems from their unfair expectations of others. I had a client relate to me that he often gets extremely angry because people take advantage of him. When I asked how, he gave me some enlightening tales. He felt entitled. He was filled with an expectation that others were going to do for him equally, as he has done for them. When they didn't follow through as he expected, it caused him to be angry. Did he communicate his expectation to these people? No, but he lamented that they should have known. Does this sound familiar?

When an expectation is not communicated and agreed upon, it becomes an unfair expectation. In a marital situation, these unfair expectations occur all the time between husbands and wives. With children, parents deliver these unfair expectations frequently.

Supervisors place these expectations on their employees. It seems that people expect you to read their minds. This is extremely unfair.

Have you ever loaned someone money that was never paid back? What was it that got you upset? If you get to the real issue it was because you lent this person money with the expectation, they would return the loan. If the repayment wasn't communicated then it is an unfair expectation.

How Personality Types Affect Assertiveness

There are several different personality types: They are Passive, Passive-Aggressive, Aggressive, Alternator, and Assertive. Let's look at each one and see which most closely resembles your behavior.

Beliefs of a PASSIVE personality	
Being Assertive means being selfish and mean	If I am passive I'll be loved
I am worthwhile only when I please others	It's not polite to disagree
I must be wrong if people disagree with me	I must be nice at all times
I have no opinions because mine don't matter	

Beliefs of a PASSIVE-AGGRESSIVE personality	
People should be more considerate	I would be Assertive but I am afraid of failing.

Beliefs of an AGGRESSIVE personality	
I have the right to be angry!	I have to be Aggressive in order to get things done
Everyone is out to get me!	

Personality types are a good clue as to how you feel and relate to yourself. You relate to yourself by means of automatic thoughts, which bring about self-talk. Therefore, if these thoughts are of an affirmative nature, your self-talk will be positive. However, if it is of a negative base, your self-talk will likely be self-destructive and negative.

It is extremely important to examine what you tell yourself and institute some positive changes if needed. If negative, this behavior is harmful to every aspect of your life and your relationships.

Self-Therapy or Self-Talk ━━━━━━━━━━━━━━━━━━━━━

In Psychology, there is a practice called self-therapy, which sometimes is referred to as self-talk. When used properly, this practice can help increase self-esteem, confidence, and self-worth. It is also used in the practice of rehearsal. The most common type of self-therapy used is negative. It is telling yourself that you are bad, stupid, worthless, no good, too fat, too skinny, or ugly, etc. Most people were never taught to do this to themselves, they just automatically do it.

Self-therapy or self-talk is used all the time, specifically when stress, anxiety, frustration, or a domestic violence situation is present. Unfortunately, the negative aspect of self-therapy is the one that usually appears.

Note: I found that within this phenomenon referred to as self-therapy or self-talk, we continue to beat ourselves up with dialogue that has been handed down to us by our parents, teachers, the media, our peers, and so on. This dialogue is made up of specific terms and phrases such as, try, hope, if, fail, can't, but, should, must, should have, I ought to have, must have, plus many more. These are some of the self-abusive terms we use on ourselves daily.

I would like to share my personal point of view of these terms and ask that you please have an open mind. These words and phrases do a couple of things; first they are used to give you an escape, or an excuse to keep from taking responsibility for your own actions and decisions.

By using these excuses, we stay firmly planted and ignore what really needs to be done. Further, we teach our children to refrain from taking responsibility for their actions and decisions, ultimately teaching them to lie. Aren't you lying to your children when you don't follow through with something you've told them?

The negative process of "self-talk" is used to degrade and put yourself down. This way you are validating those contradictory thoughts and beliefs others have placed on you, and you pick up where they left off. These particular words are very damaging.

Phrases used such as, *"should have, I ought to have, and must have"* keep you from giving yourself the freedom of choice. This puts unfair expectations on yourself with no way out. When you don't succeed, your negative beliefs are substantiated and the old tapes begin to play and increase, thereby perpetuating the cognitive distortions and automatic thoughts that have continued to hurt you.

I dislike the word *"try."* Try to stand from a sitting position. Did you *try* or did you do it? Try is one of those words thoughtlessly used on a consistent basis, without any consideration as to how it will influence your children, not to mention how it is subliminally affecting you. Either you are going to do it, or you are not, but you are not going to *"try."* You will make an attempt; to what degree you'll make that attempt is your choice. When you begin to change your self-talk to be more positive, your thought processes begin to change for the better and your influence becomes more beneficial.

The word *"hope"* is another word that gives you a bit of disappointment because of the way it is often used. If used in reference to others, it then is used appropriately. However, if used in reference to yourself, it leaves room for doubt. Wouldn't it be better to say, *"I would like for this to happen, however if it doesn't, I'll be okay."* This gives you the flexibility to choose and you can feel good about coming back for another attempt at success.

"If" is another one of those words that gives false hope about things you have little or no chance of attaining. *"If I win the lotto, then...."* This word brings with it disappointment. Don't you have enough disappointment in your life?

"Can't" is a word that is consistently used incorrectly. Accurately speaking, can't means you are *"incapable"* of doing something. We use it to lie to our kids and other people. It is better to be up front and honest. We say we can't, when we really mean we

don't want to, or we prefer not to. We teach our children how to use excuses and to manipulate with words.

"But" is an interesting word. Think for a moment of how people use this word in every sentence they utter. My personal opinion is that "but" really means to, **forget what I just said and believe me now.** This word is used to avoid staying focused on a particular issue and is also used to confuse the listener. Listen very carefully... When talking with someone, pay attention to how and when they use this word. The more excited they are, the more they will use it. When you begin to realize what they are doing, you are better able to maintain your focus. By asking them not to use this word, it does not allow them to sidetrack from the issue, which may frustrate them.

Another way "but" is used may hit home with some of you. When someone apologizes for something, very often the word, but, enters into the apology. What this person is doing is offering an excuse for their bad behavior, or they are attempting to divert responsibility. When one has been caught doing something wrong, and they are attempting to offer an explanation for their actions, yet again, but is used to offer excuses or a reason for their actions. The word but is used to mitigate the severity of their mistake. Now stop and think for a moment, is but ever used when forgiveness is asked for? No! No one wants to mitigate their request for forgiveness, do they? For example: I am really sorry ... please forgive me, but... This rarely happens and when it does, it is a wishy-washy offer of forgiveness, not a true apology. "But" is used to minimize or sidestep.

The word I dislike and find to be the most harmful word in our language is, failure! Of all the people I have dealt with in my practice and throughout my life, I can not count the number of times failure has been used in conversations with me. It has always been a negative. If it is true that we only control ourselves and how people and situations affect us, then how can you fail at something you cannot control? When it comes to yourself, you still do not fail, because people choose to give up or quit; they don't choose to fail! Therefore, failure does not exist unless you want it to; that is your choice!

Think for a moment about one thing that you have failed at. Do you have it? I have found that people will either give up or quit; they do not fail. There is nothing wrong with quitting or giving up when every possible avenue has been challenged, or the person simply has no desire to continue. I know there are people that will be shocked or upset with my point of view, and it is okay.

I can't think of one thing in my life in which I have ever failed. I have made my share of bad decisions and choices, and I have learned from them all. The use of that negative word is for the control and manipulation of others.

In our educational system, children are placed in competition against all other children in the same age group. They are judged by how they did or did not do, physically and academically within that group. The letter grade system we currently have bears those results. If that child does work inconsistent with national standards, and it is low enough, they are considered to be failing and are labeled a failure, which will follow them the rest of their lives. If nothing is done to intervene, the child will eventually begin to believe they are a failure, and will question themselves about why they should continue to try. Whether we find the reason for the low grade or not, I find the usage of this term to be unacceptable. I would prefer to see no grade or credit rather than an "F" for failing.

There are other terms that may reflect the deficiency which has less harmful effects on children and adults. For instance, instead of telling a child they failed, how about reframing it to, "Tommy, it seems as though you are having some difficulty; what can we do together to help you," or, "Tommy, after reviewing your exam you have fallen short of attaining a satisfactory level, what is it you are having trouble with?" This way you are communicating that he has done poorly and that he has someone in his corner to help.

Wouldn't this be more motivating and less harmful than putting a label of failure on him?

This term failure is unfair, and it certainly is not helpful to anyone. In fact, it is particularly damaging to a child, especially for a child with a learning disability. It can also be damaging to those from different ethnic backgrounds, those with a low self-esteem or confidence level, or those who come from an emotionally and/or physically abusive home. If they do not or cannot achieve what society believes is *normal*, they have failed. If that concept is true, then every man, woman and child on this planet is a failure in one way or another! By damaging one's self-esteem and labeling them a failure how can this possibly be a positive motivator for them to meet someone else's expectations? It is important to consider all the child's personal characteristics and influences, such as ethnicity, home life, possibility of learning disabilities, etc.

The letter grade system needs to be revamped. A more effective system would be a pass or no pass system, where the children would be in competition only with themselves.

If you were raised with this *"failure"* concept as a child, you carry those scars into adulthood, and you may never understand why. The older you are, the more difficult it is to face that hurdle and overcome it, and the less desire you have to change. One thing is for certain, if the problem is not identified and acknowledged, it cannot be fixed!

As a boy growing up, I was constantly hearing teachers and my parents talk about how stupid

I was...how slow I was. After the other students heard these comments, I was left to deal with their ridicule, and you know how mean children can be. My self-esteem and confidence level took a nose-dive and I learned to hate school and myself.

Many times I overheard discussions about me being a candidate for the special education program because I had extreme difficulty with math and reading. My desire to learn died due to the embarrassment and hatred I felt for my parents, school, teachers, my peers, and for myself.

I was never approached about finding a reason for my difficulties; I was only approached about failing. I was always told the same dialogue, *"if you don't try harder, you're going to fail! You'll never amount to anything. Do you want to be a failure all of your life? Stop being lazy, or you're going to fail!"* This was very upsetting and damaging to me. I have seen the same issues in the lives of my clients. In society this situation is shrugged off and people are told to get over it, or they are ignored and find themselves stuck in low paying, menial jobs. This is unjust; however, we are the only ones that can initiate change.

It is vitally important for parents, teachers, and society to be very aware of how their words are being used and how they are affecting children and themselves. It is essential for people to use terms and phrases that are up-building and encouraging. Parents, teachers, and society do not have the right to downgrade or belittle our children, others, or ourselves. Remember, we cannot give our child that which we do not possess!

There is one big exception. Have you ever heard the saying, *"We don't plan to fail, we fail to plan?"* Other than I don't believe in the term, *"failure,"* that statement has a great deal of truth. I do believe that you cannot succeed if you don't make the appropriate choices or decisions. In other words, if you avoid making a decision because you say you need time to think and allow that decision to go by the way side, you didn't fail, you simply decided wrong. By not making a decision, you made one anyway.

If you are afraid to make a decision because of uncertainty, or because you selfishly want something or someone you have no control over, then you will most likely not do the right thing.

Remember, all people, as well as children, learn primarily by what they "see" not by what they hear. Therefore, be prudent with your time, energy, and the use of your logical decision-making skills. In difficult times, it will help if you separate your feelings and emotions from your logic, and examine the facts before making your decision. This is a great stress reliever.

Self-talk or self-therapy is a very important concept that can have extremely favorable results, if utilized properly. Those results have a direct effect on your children and everyone in your world. Please strongly consider this section.

DEPRESSION

This section does nothing more than perpetuate negative self-talk. I believe depression is okay and can be healthy from time to time. However, it will become a problem if and when you get stuck there. This is why it is so important to listen to your body and be aware of any symptoms, both of depression or other unusual feelings.

The majority of self-talk people use comes from feelings of depression and is usually negative in nature. Depression comes from feelings of inadequacy, helplessness, and worthlessness, feelings of being abused, and feeling that your life is spiraling out of control. You feel that you are incapable of succeeding in what you do, or that you can't achieve what you want. Depression can be created by the negative thoughts and beliefs of others that you have adopted for your own. This can be a never-ending, vicious circle, unless you choose to find an appropriate way to stop it. This is somewhat simplified but nonetheless, accurate.

It is very important to learn to be aware of your body and what is going on with it; learn to read it. For instance, I have been CPR trained most of my life, and I knew the symptoms of a heart attack. When I had my heart attack several years ago, it was not like anything I had ever heard or read about. I simply experienced a sore throat, nothing more. I did, however, know that something was wrong. I listened to my body and what it was telling me; is that I needed to act! I didn't completely understand, so I had to seek out some answers. With the help of my wife, I soon found out that I was experiencing a heart attack. The rest is history, and

I am thankful I listened and chose to seek help. Even more so, I am grateful for having a loving wife that was caring enough to help me.

If you are experiencing hopelessness, low self-esteem, low self-worth, and feeling down on yourself and your life, there is a good possibility you might be experiencing depression. You might experience the feeling of having no interest in anything, being fatigued or confused, and numb of feelings and emotions. You might experience distorted thinking, feeling that your life is falling apart. You may experience irregular eating or sleeping patterns, weight fluctuation, and the arrival of self-destructive behaviors, such as alcohol or drug usage, and of course the increased ritual of negative self-talk. You might experience physical and/or emotional isolation, where you don't feel like going anywhere or doing anything. I have known people with depression so severe they became bed ridden and locked themselves in their bedroom.

If you become aware of depression and the effects and causes, you'll have the ability to deal with it, provided you are committed to and accept responsibility for your actions, thoughts, and behaviors. The cognitive distortions we just discussed have helped create your depression, and by committing yourself to change those distortions, you will live a happier, healthier life.

Learn the tools in this book to regain your control and self-efficacy, in other words, take back your personal power. Understand that your value, happiness, and success do not depend on the opinions and beliefs of others. It solely depends on what you think and feel about yourself.

Helplessness is founded on what you do not do, not what you are doing. Use the tools in this book to learn to trust yourself again. Independence is trusting in your feelings, thoughts, and decisions, and in your personal control. Use positive self-talk to support and validate yourself and gather around you those individuals that will support the development of your self-empowerment. Those individuals would be the people that truly care about you; it is important that you make yourself one of them! Care about your own personal well being!!

Forget about who you *"should be, or ought to be,"* and begin thinking about the person you know you *can* be. Get rid of the negative terms from your vocabulary we discussed earlier. Stop pretending to be what others want you to be. By accomplishing this, you will gain a certain amount of calm, confidence, and happiness. Be honest with yourself and others, even if it hurts, and utilize your reciprocal boundaries. Admit and accept the fact that you are human and are going to make mistakes. It is okay as long as you learn from them.

Utilize your personal rights and don't feel bad, guilty, or shameful for doing so. Learn to effectively communicate your feelings, thoughts, ideas, and displeasures, etc. It is important to note that those who are afraid to speak their feelings and express their anger are the ones falling prey to depression and worse.

Learn the tools to deal with your past so you won't find any reason to live there. *Bad things happen to good people.* You are a good person that has been misguided and misinformed about yourself. The distorted thoughts and beliefs from childhood have hardened you and caused you to feel bad about yourself. These negative feelings create depression. Depression has instituted a measure of dysfunction and chaos in your life toward yourself and others. It is important you learn to forgive... Forgiveness is for you, not for those who have hurt you.

Learn what your personal and environmental needs are because these are essential to keep your life in balance. It is also important to keep your personal rights in mind while working to achieve a life balance. Depression can be dealt with successfully. It is not easy, but it is do-able.

What would you like to do, now?

Gender Issues

WOMEN

Everyone has heard of the *"generation gap."* Parents and their children have experienced this phenomenon for centuries. This usually causes extreme chaos and may cause a division in the family. One of the most damaging effects of the generation gap is finger pointing and placing blame. Finger pointing and placing blame never creates a positive outcome; it only creates negativity and destruction for those involved. People who finger point and place blame on others do this to avoid taking responsibility and accountability for their own actions. This has stumped people for years. I believe this to be nothing more than a communication problem between some parents and their children. Included in the act of communicating is active listening, understanding, and respecting one's reality. I refer to this "generation gap" as nothing more than a *communication* gap. Neither of these has learned how to effectively communicate and actively listen, hence the *gap*. The act of effective communication has always been left up to the child to learn on the streets, and when the child picks up the language of the streets, parents and adults are dumbfounded. They get upset because they have no idea what their child is saying and likewise, the child experiences difficulty understanding the parents.

There is another phenomena that exists between men and women; I refer to this as the *"gender gap."* This has been around even longer than the generation gap. This usually brings with it the same affect that the generation gap brings. In reality, there are no gaps, these are just tag names or labels that society puts on things they can't explain or have little or no desire to figure out. There is a severe lack of effective communication in the world, as well, there is a lack of education about how to appropriately communicate. As in everything else, there are rules, techniques and tools people need to be aware of in order to facilitate an effective communication. Examining these tools and techniques, it becomes more easily understood, which enables us to resolve the problems more effectively.

These communication gaps exist because of the way men and women are raised and the life experiences that influenced their core beliefs. These core beliefs become rigidly instilled in each person. We can not forget that society has a responsibility in this, as well. Understandably, there is a great difference between men and women. Remember, I stated earlier that understanding is one major key to our existence. If we can understand this and accept the information, we will be able to make some great changes in our relationships. Keep in mind that it is extremely easy to rationalize and justify your behavior, thoughts, and feelings. If we do rationalize these things, it will counter everything we have done thus far.

Question: What are some of the problems women experience?

Generally, women are raised to have passive behaviors and attitudes. Women are raised to believe they are responsible for serving others as well as for the happiness of their family members and others. The guidance they get usually comes from the "demands" of others. This too is instilled in women that they should be nice, meaning that women should never, ever say, "no" nor should they ever disagree.

Women are indoctrinated with the belief that they are going to be measured by the success of their relationships. This, of course, is a myth that needs to be expelled. What this is saying to women is that they are required to do anything and everything possible to make their mate happy and content, and only then will they be successful. This means you are not going to disagree with anything he says or does.

Further, the woman will not communicate her negative feelings or any kind of displeasure she feels and will not place any kind of demands or requests on him. What it boils down to is women are expected to cook, clean, do the washing, be his sex partner, nurse, caretaker, eye candy, maid, errand girl, and whatever else he wants. It is also expected that you will not give any rebuttal to this process… What a crock! Do not fall into this lifestyle because it is extremely difficult to get out. Women who have a fear of ending up alone, or fear that no one wants them because they might have children or because of their age, is nonsense. If you believe in yourself and love yourself, you will seldom feel that you *NEED* someone.

You need to get to a place in your life where you *WANT* some-one. There is a big difference. If you love yourself, you will be happy with yourself and with God. Remember, everything in life is a choice…a personal choice. You can choose to live in a horrible relationship or to be happy and content. You do not have to live with abuse of any kind. I would prefer to live alone rather than tolerate physical or emotional abuse! What would you prefer?

Women are raised to be nurturers, caretakers, maids, and cooks as their familial responsibility. Along with these, they are taught to use their feelings and emotions to make decisions and problem-solve. In the workplace, women are expected to take a back seat to men when it comes to positioning and income. Al-though unspoken, women are viewed socially as being unequal to men, which are cognitive distortions. Distortions like these are extremely damaging to one's self-esteem and confidence. These ideologies assist in creating fear and hesitation, and force women into a passive and submissive personality type.

MEN

Question: What are some of the problems men experience?

Men have been taught to have no sense of self. In other words, they are the breadwinners, and they have to be selfless for others. Men are not expected to really have any personal interests. They require no nurturing because they are supposed to be a *"rock."*

Men are taught to believe that they are physically and emo-tionally tough. One sign of weakness is to be overwhelmed by work. The result is an inability to say no, resulting in an unreasonable workload. Many times because of these distortions, men become "workaholics." Do you know any men like this? They are raised to have "macho" attitudes and are guided by their own ego and masculinity, instead of by common sense and sensitivities.

They are raised to believe that talking about their feelings and emotions is a sign of ultimate weakness. My brother and other men I have talked with refer to my profession as "touchy-feely" nonsense. Most men are "fearful" to admit being afraid of things, especially if it relates to feelings and emotions. In many cases, their fear translates into anger, isolation, the use of alcohol or drugs, or all the above.

They believe "a real man" has to be aggressive, pushy, and demanding to get what he wants or needs. It is a sign of weakness to ask, to compromise, or to commit. They believe they need to control others and they refuse to admit it. Many men adopt a philosophy of "it's my way or the highway." They were raised to be overbearing and expect passive obedience from others.

When a child attempts any form of assertiveness they usually are struck down physically and/or emotionally. Many times this causes the child to be fearful of true assertiveness and to resent authority. Any attempts by their spouse to be assertive will typically result in angering the male. Through this type of indoctrination, these men wear these beliefs as a type of "armor" and are fearful of being found out. If these fears are discovered, they may isolate emotionally and their relationships, children, and jobs are damaged; every aspect of their lives may be negatively altered. The issues that have been discussed so far are so very important to your personal, professional, and intimate relationships and to your growth.

Most men find it difficult to make a commitment or communicate effectively with women.

They either find it unnecessary or believe it to be a sign of weakness and refuse to engage in meaningful discussions. When this occurs; there is usually an argument that ensues, at the very least problems begin to arise in the relationship. The strongest man in the world was the most sensitive; he was Jesus Christ.

SOCIAL

Question: How does society play into our beliefs, relationships, and behaviors?

This is an interesting and curious question. For generations, social influence has been part of our lives. These include schools, the judicial system, churches, media, film, music, books, magazines, newspapers, our family members, the general public, as well as our friends… these have a strong direct influence on our lives. They influence what we think, feel, and believe. They influence how we make decisions, and have a straightforward impact on our problem solving abilities and how we communicate. They influence every aspect of our lives. Social influence is the icing on the cake, so to speak. However, if we utilize the concepts discussed in this book, the social influences can be used appropriately to benefit our lives and relationships.

The effects of society is one section of influence, and is not totally responsible for the impact on a person. It's the combined responsible effort of all areas of society used to educate and supply a child's required needs. To pick just one area and state that this is the main cause of bad behavior and attitude is unequivocally wrong.

I believe it is the responsibility of everyone to oversee all areas of a child's life and their activities. It is important to have some idea where the pitfalls are to protect themselves and their children. Everyone in society has an unquestionable responsibility to be proactive in their personal lives, as well as the lives of their children. Sadly enough, this too is one's choice! Let's briefly look at each area.

From birth, we are indoctrinated with mom and dad's beliefs, morals, values, ideologies, and world views about many aspects of life. Considering that we are all imperfect, many parent's beliefs, morals, values, ideologies, and world views are going to be distorted, in one way or another. These are the ones that need to be scrutinized in depth, because they are the ones that will cause us lifelong grief.

I was raised in a family that was, in my opinion, very prejudice toward minorities. These beliefs were then and continue to be horribly wrong, but they were the beliefs of my step-father. Whether he intended to pass them on to us or not, we were still indoctrinated with those particular beliefs. When you view others with similar beliefs, you can't help but notice the destruction it causes.

The distorted beliefs and behaviors children have learned become the catalyst for their relationships. These friendships validate one another's beliefs and behaviors, regardless of the level of distortion. Isn't it true that misery loves company?

Years ago, I held the position of Security Specialist for a local middle school. It was an above average income area, with many political influences. I noticed disturbing activities going on, and I soon become aware of the causes for these inappropriate behaviors. I'd like to share a couple of those situations with you. These had a direct influence on many children and when brought to the attention of the proper authorities, they were either dismissed or swept under the carpet.

I was inspecting the school one afternoon, and I noticed a young boy sitting in the hallway, sobbing. When asked why he was crying, he related that he was asked to leave the class because of his rudeness and disruptive behavior with the other students. He went on to explain that his family was transferred here from South America. His father was an engineer on a Government project. His native language was Spanish, and he spoke with broken English.

The reason he was upset was that he wanted to learn English because he already spoke fluent

Spanish. The school and teachers ignored his request and placed him in a Spanish class. I found out later that the English teacher didn't want to take on that challenge, so she demanded that he be put in a Spanish class to make things easier for her, giving no consideration to the student. When this was brought to the attention of the proper authorities, it was ignored and the student was required to remain in the Spanish class. The irony of this was when I listened to chit chat in the teacher's lounge, they were often complaining that *"these"* kids can't speak English. They refused to teach a student who really wanted to learn, because it was too difficult. This child developed resentments and was ridiculed by the other students and the teacher.

Another instance that took place was when the school began to bus lower income students into the school, many of which were Hispanic. It is important to note that not all these lower income children were affiliated with gangs. I found a few of the boys were treated as though they were gang members simply because of their culture and ethnicity and the way they dressed. Worst of all, because of the perception of a fearful teacher, these boys were forced to defend their lifestyle, their culture, and even their ethnicity. What influence do you think this had on those boys? I believe these irresponsible teachers and staff violated these young students! Do you think the actions of the teachers and staff validated the suspicions and mistrust these minorities had learned at home? I do! This happens daily at church, on the streets, in restaurants and almost every place you go. This is why it is so important to be proactive and to be involved in all aspects of your child's life. The daily hurts and traumas that occur with kids assist in creating cognitive distortions in them, and if not intervened, may cause permanent damage later in life. What are your thoughts? Does this remind you of any childhood hurts?

One final example is of an 8th grade girl who was stomped and kicked by several boys while on school property. She was beaten up because she refused to have sex with her boyfriend, who was one of the boys kicking her. She was in the hospital for several days, and this act of violence was swept under the carpet. The girl came from a lower income family and these boys were from affluent backgrounds with highly influential families. This girl was horribly traumatized, and may possibly suffer lifelong effects. Who will take responsibility to protect the victims in these situations and who will accept the responsibility for these children's bad behaviors and attitudes in future years? Do you think as young adults and even into adulthood, someone will step up and accept the responsibility for these people? I think not. Rest assured that their bad behaviors and attitudes will be the sole focus, and the causalities will be ignored.

Let's look at the media. Before continuing, I want to clarify that I do not believe it is appropriate to ban, burn, or allow the destruction of books. However, I do believe with every ounce of my being, that we have a responsibility to be proactive and guide our youth in the proper understanding of all material viewed, heard, and read.

I do not believe that through the simple act of watching a movie, listening to a piece of music, or by reading a book can cause one to act out violently. However, I do believe in conjunction with one's learned life experiences, the messages received through these forms of media can create a powerful influence.

Look at Columbine High School in April 1999. These boys had many psychological issues before committing this tragedy; unfortunately for the victims, these signs were ignored. I believe they received specific ideas and thoughts as to how they should carry out this atrocity. I also believe they received some form of validation for what they were about to do.

When we look at violence and explicit sex acted out in films and TV, and the violence and disrespect toward women, verbally spoken in music and written about in books and magazines, I don't find it difficult to ask why this person has such an offensive and destructive behavior. Instead, I have to ask why not? As a society, we have allowed and enabled this type of behavior to be perpetuated by being *"reactive."* By not accepting responsibility, not being involved with our children's lives, and not giving proper guidance to what they watch, read, and listen to, society has helped create the bad behaviors and attitudes. We can't simply sidestep their behaviors and attitudes by saying, *"I did the best I could, or they are just out of control."* Excuses like these are placing blame and pointing fingers; this doesn't wash any longer. It is easier for society to look at a child's bad behavior, and crucify the child and ignore the causality.

The result of allowing this type of entertainment in movies, music, books, and so on, is that children and adults are becoming more and more desensitized to the needs of others, as well as their own needs. This is wrong and needs to be stopped!

It is time to be *PROACTIVE* and accept responsibility for how our children are being raised and what they learn. Do not sit idly by and expect that children will learn what they need to on the streets; it doesn't work that way. Do not depend on others to take your responsibility to raise, guide, and teach your children what is required to live a happy healthy life. Take a moment and reflect on your own childhood to see if you can discover what has contributed to your issues.

Question: After what you have read thus far, what conclusions have you come up with concerning your own behaviors, beliefs, and relationships? What are some of the influences that you have had? Are you satisfied with your life and relationships? If not, what are you willing to do to change it?

Dr. Phil McGraw says that one can't fix what they don't acknowledge. I completely agree with this. Therefore, if you examine those problem areas in your life, apply the tools in this book, and write them down, you'll be more empowered to fix them. Keep in mind that you do not want to rationalize or justify these areas.

Remember, many of the beliefs preventing us from being assertive are in our own heads. They are the fears we were indoctrinated with throughout our formative years. Those negative beliefs represent our own distorted views of the world and of ourselves.

We are the only one in control of our behaviors and beliefs, and others are in control of theirs.

Note: As a boy, I was instructed about what I should believe about women and relationships. Those descriptions really identify how I was raised, which was to dislike, mistrust, and to believe that women were only out to use me.

I have a bad habit of asking questions. I also seem to have an obsession about finding out why people act and react the way they do, which leads to an understanding why my family seemed to be so dysfunctional and screwed up. This desire that burned inside of me, helped me to see the reality of my own life and of myself.

Many men, including my brothers, tell me that this *"therapy crap"* is nothing but a waste of time and that people should be able to fix their own problems instead of paying someone to help them. I've been told that it is only the weak-minded, lazy, or the self-pitying person that needs therapy. I believe this is why so many people are stuck in their past traumas, where they continue to live today.

Both of my brothers are good mechanics. Should someone with little or no knowledge about car repair, such as I, be expected to fix my car by myself, or should I be smart enough to pay someone who knows how to fix it, and save myself some time and aggravation?

It is the same thing with feelings, emotions, and the individual ghosts that haunt each of us. Do we simply ignore them and hope they go away or do we make a feeble attempt to fix them ourselves with little or no knowledge about the process? Do we take a huge chance of making things worse, or do we find someone with the ability and knowledge to help us? If the answer is to fix it themselves, this shows me a destructive ego. This is likened to the criminal who represents himself in court; he has a fool for a client.

It is not a sign of weakness to seek therapy or any kind of help.

In reality, it is a sign of inner strength and respect for themselves and their family members. Ridiculing others for seeking therapy means the ridiculer has issues and does not know how to deal with them effectively. My best advice is to ignore these types of individuals and proceed. Focus on what is necessary and important for you to develop your own personal coat of armor. There is no time like the present to accept and own responsibility for your own life and the lives of your children.

"Every decision you make today will
follow you the rest of your life."

~Lee Braddock~

CHAPTER **4**

Developing Emotional Body Armor

"We teach people how to treat us." How do you like to be treated?

Reciprocal Boundaries

In my career, I am constantly asked, what exactly are boundaries? How can I set my boundaries or figure out what boundaries I need to set? Where do I begin? These questions come up regularly. I have attended numerous seminars and read many books, including self-help books, and other material where the subject of boundaries is brought up. It is unfortunate that these materials rarely address the above specific questions. We are simply told that we need to set our boundaries. Of course, if you ask someone if they have boundaries, they usually will reply with, *"yes, I do,"* when in reality, they may not.

In family therapy, couples therapy, pre-marital therapy, victims abuse therapy, addiction therapy, and in general wellness, the subject of *"boundaries"* frequently comes up. The commonality is that there is rarely an explanation of what boundaries are, and far less often is the clarification provided to explain how and why to use them. If you don't understand the complete concept of what boundaries are and how to implement them, there is a good chance you will create chaos in your life and relationships. This occurs not only in one's personal life, but I see it occurring in one's professional life as well.

Lastly, people are NOT taught how to defend themselves in an assertive way. Boys, for instance, are expected to get physical and women are expected to simply "settle." In every case, I have found the lack of boundaries create problematic areas in the lives of most people.

The term boundaries are loosely used and generally misunderstood. It is apparent to me that in dealing with clients and people in general, they behave as though boundaries are meant for everyone but them. In the real world, boundaries are for our personal protection. They are for everyone, including the person that set them. On the other hand, I have found many people who believe they *have* set their boundaries and when others violate them...they are upset, and unfortunately, do not enforce the consequences of violating the boundary.

Let's examine the term, *"boundary;"* what does it mean? For the sake of time and simplicity, a boundary is something that indicates a *"fixed limit or to a fixed degree."*

There are different areas in which boundaries need to be placed. As well, there are diverse categories of boundaries; i.e. personal, familial, and professional. Boundaries are the *"armor"* we need to protect ourselves and our families.

Boundaries are used to protect our emotions, feelings, relationships, and our physical person. The sad reality is that society, parents, schools, and churches have not taught these concepts. As with alcohol, drugs, sex, and effective communication, these too, are never taught, but they are all taken for granted and left up the individual to learn from wherever they may. That's a big mistake and a huge injustice for our children, as well as for us!

I feel the term, boundaries, does not quite fit our means. I refer to boundaries as *"Reciprocal Boundaries."* The term reciprocal means, *"mutual, give and take, shared, or equal"* and we know what boundaries mean. When reciprocal boundaries are put into place and enforced, we have created a wonderful suit of armor for ourselves. This will help you teach people how to treat you in an appropriate way, if you commit to setting and enforcing them.

How does this armor emerge? You have personal *rights;* do you know what those rights are? Your individual reciprocal boundaries emerge from our acknowledgment and acceptance of our personal rights... in general, you have a right to be yourself and to take care of yourself, which is also your personal responsibility! You need to learn to value, trust, respect, and listen to yourselves and understand what your rights and needs are. It is important to believe in your rights and needs, what you like, dislike, what you believe in and what you deserve to have in life. Many people have said we need to do these things, but it has not been explained to most of us how to accomplish this task and why we should do it.

What does it mean to set our reciprocal boundaries? Setting reciprocal boundaries means you are going to make decisions for yourselves, and commit to accepting responsibility for your personal actions, thoughts, and behaviors. It means you command respect and equality from the people around you, whether it be a family member, friend, co-worker, spouse, or someone else!

By setting our boundaries, we have accepted the responsibility of taking care of ourselves and giving ourselves permission to say *"no"* to those things that are *NOT* for us or our family. These boundaries are an assertive way of defending our personal rights.

The word *"no"* holds unlimited power and has a wonderful affect on us. Although, we must be aware of the consequences, if we are in an abusive relationship, it could cause a spouse or significant other to become angry or even violent. We cannot allow this to deter us from our goals. We should be proactive and arrange to protect ourselves and our children.

Everyone possesses personal rights and those rights need to be protected. The discovery and development of your boundaries begin with these rights. If we don't know what our rights are, we're not going to be able to properly and effectively put our boundaries in place.

We all have constitutional rights that cover many areas of our lives. However, they do not cover all of our *personal* rights. As adults, it is our responsibility to learn about our rights and teach them to our children.

The following list are some of our personal rights you may want to consider. Which of these do you use? Which do you not? Why, or why not? As you go through this list, write down the ones that are important to you.

PERSONAL RIGHTS

1. I have a right to ask for what I want.
2. I have a right to say no to requests or demands that I cannot meet, do not desire, feel I am not ready for, is unsafe, or conflicts with my values, morals, or lifestyle.
3. I have a right to express my feelings—positive or negative.
4. I have a right to change my mind.
5. I have a right to make mistakes and do not have to be perfect.
6. I have a right to follow my own values and beliefs.
7. I have the right to determine my own priorities.
8. I have the right NOT to be responsible for the actions, feelings, or behaviors of others, including my spouse or significant other.
9. I have the right to expect honesty from others
10. I have the right to be angry at someone I love.
11. I have the right to be myself and to be unique.
12. I have the right to express my fears.
13. I have the right to say, "I don't know."
14. I have the right NOT to explain my behavior.
15. I have the right to make my own decisions, based on whatever I choose.
16. I have the right to my own personal space and time.
17. I have a right to speak my displeasures.

18. I have the right to be emotionally healthy and happy.
19. I have the right to feel safe, and be in a non-abusive environment and relationship.
20. I have the right to make friends and be comfortable around people.
21. I have the right to change and grow.
22. I have the right to have my wants and needs respected by others.
23. I have the right to be treated with dignity and respect.
24. I have a right to love and be loved.

If you are not confident about your personal rights, take time to read this list daily until you do become confident and begin to assimilate them into your lifestyle. After you have done that, begin to create your boundaries to protect those rights you feel most passionate about. It may be helpful to post a copy of these where you have the opportunity to see them often for reinforcement.

Self-talk is also very helpful to build up confidence and trust in yourself. Some of my clients made laminated cards and carry their list of rights everywhere. On occasion, they would relate to me that they have had conversations with family and friends about their personal rights, and they requested a copy for themselves. If you think of more rights, you should write those down, too.

When you choose to take that major step and commit to change, and you begin to overcome your fears and learn the concepts, tools, and techniques of assertiveness, then you will begin to create, nurture, and maintain strong, healthy relationships. The relationships I am referring to are two types. They are **inter**personal-relationships, which involves others in our life, and the other is **intra**personal relationships. This is the most important one and should take priority, because this relationship is the one you have with yourself. It is very important to understand that we cannot give something to others that we do not possess ourselves. Example: If you don't possess self-respect, you can't give respect to others and expect to receive it in return. If you don't possess respect for yourself, how can you teach your children to respect themselves?

Look at it from this standpoint; if you allow your physical health to deteriorate, and you become bedridden, your mental health also begins to deteriorate. Your mental and physical health are two of your required needs for a balanced life. How can you give your children their needs of physical and mental health if you are bedridden with illness? It is not possible. You have to be healthy to ensure their health.

Once you begin this wonderfully scary and exciting journey, you are going to experience one heck

of a boost to your self-esteem, confidence, and sense of self. You'll experience some traumatic times as well, because we all have those areas in our past that we would much rather forget. We never want to forget them, but we do want to learn from them.

You'll begin to see changes in your lifestyle, relationships with family members, and people who have known you for some time. When you begin this journey, you will see very quickly and clearly who truly does care for you, and who does not. The people you see that don't care about you, are the ones you need to exclude from your life, by means of your boundaries. This may include family members, friends, adult children, co-workers, and even your boss.

You'll also begin to see wonderful results from new relationships you will create. These will be more satisfying and complete, because you'll be teaching these people how to treat you, in a manner which respects you and your boundaries. You might conclude that you don't "need" anyone (a man or woman) in your life right now, but rather that you "want" someone in your life; this is a huge difference… It is called independence.

You will see and feel your anger, rage, your whining, and feelings of being threatened or emotionally smothered. Feelings of being a victim will greatly diminish. Assertiveness brings forth the feelings of "personal independence and freedom." The more independent and free you feel, the more you'll want to venture out into the world for new discoveries and the more you'll want to learn.

STRATEGIES FOR SETTING YOUR RECIPROCAL BOUNDARIES

I mentioned, The Assertiveness Workbook by Dr. Randy Paterson, wherein he refers to the Bonsai Principle, meaning, *"keep it short, simple and to the point."* After figuring out what your boundaries will be, you need to understand 3 things.

A. **Effective Communication**: You need to communicate what your boundaries are in a clear, concise, and understandable fashion. You also need confirmation that this person clearly understands those boundaries. This is done by Q & A with that person.

B. **Consequences**: There has to be a consequence when others violate your boundaries, which also must be communicated.

C. **Enforcement**: If your boundaries are violated, you must enforce them by following through with the consequence you communicated, regardless of your relationship with the violator.

Important Tool: Before you communicate with anyone, always, always, *"rehearse"* what you need to say, and how you want to say it, so you feel confident, comfortable, and self-assured. This is the beginning of teaching people how to treat you. When you do, you will begin to command respect from others and you will feel self-respected. This rehearsal needs to be done *aloud* so that you can hear what you are saying and how you are saying it.

What is the difference between "Command and Demand when referring to respect?"

- When you command respect, you gain respect by your actions or positive influence.
- If you demand respect, you are telling people they must respect you; this is the incorrect way. Remember, the majority of communications is performed non-verbally. So

you don't necessarily have to say anything to command respect, your actions will say it for you.
- Don't feel embarrassed and don't be afraid. This is your life…your existence.
- Be prepared to defend your rights and your boundaries.

Don't be surprised when family and friends test your boundaries. Assertiveness is a new lifestyle; it will be foreign to you and to others for a while. You'll find that some people will automatically respect your boundaries and others will not. You will have a choice to make whether you want to continue a relationship with those who regularly disrespect your boundaries. Remember, when people disrespect your boundaries, they disrespect you! That choice should be a no brainer and this should be a no tolerance violation.

Do you want people in your life that do not respect your boundaries? Ask yourself if they contaminate or contribute to the relationship? Give them a choice. Remember, life is wonderful because it is a choice. Either they respect and abide by your boundaries, or they find someone else to disrespect and allow you to be happy!!

- You need a support system. Pick those people that respect you and your boundaries to have a relationship with, because they will provide your best support. You need to be part of that support system by believing in yourself.
- Don't be rushed into setting your boundaries. Be sure of what you are doing, and don't take weeks to set them in place, either. The longer it takes to set them, the less likely you are to follow through, because you'll rationalize and justify why you shouldn't follow through. Set a timetable and stick to it.
- Begin choosing and setting boundaries that are satisfying and helpful in supporting your needs for a balanced life. Use boundaries that give you the feeling of freedom, independence, and security. Write them down!

- Choose those boundaries that are going to create a person who is deserving of respect.
- Always remember as an independent individual, you possess the choice to pick your time, place to communicate, and rehearse what you need to say and how you want to say it.

Now let's look at an example of a personal boundary. These are designed for you personally. I was raised in an emotionally and physically abusive home. My boundary was that I would never be abusive to my children or my spouse. I made a personal commitment to myself and to that boundary. Remember there has to be a consequence, so the consequence that was put in place was that if I committed these acts of abuse, I would voluntarily leave the home and seek professional help for myself.

Let's look at an example of familial boundaries. These are designed for the spouse, children, and all other family members, as well as others in your life outside the workplace. For my children, it was a boundary where they could openly express their feelings, emotions, ideas, dreams, and disagreements. They were given the freedom to tell me anything they wanted. However, they had to abide by a few boundaries; they had to speak with respect, and they had to explain why, if needed. They also needed to be respectful of everyone in the household, including the house and it's property.

Boundaries between my wife and myself are simple, basic boundaries, consisting of respectful language, controlled anger, shared household responsibilities, and sharing the disciplining of the children. We agreed to never fight in front of the kids. We didn't hold secrets, we lived up to our wedding vows, and maintained a mutual respect for one another. We always maintained an open and honest communication, even during difficult times.

Let's look at an example of professional boundaries. Just as other boundaries, these need to be based on your personal rights, values, and morals. They also need to be adjusted to your work environment.

I have always made it known that my family comes first, even over my job. This is a tough one because I had to be ready to follow through with the consequences and live up to them. I have been put in a position of defending this boundary only twice, and I overcame the consequences by expressing my point of view without putting the company in harm's way. This is something to think about; I hope it helps.

THE DOWN SIDE OF BEING ASSERTIVE

Unfortunately, there is a downside to this positive and healthy lifestyle. As I said earlier, behavioral changes are the most difficult to make. The reasons are that before things get better, they usually get much worse. When starting out, you should set only those important boundaries you are actually willing to defend.

Note: Never make a threat that you are not willing or able to enforce. People will learn *NOT* to take you seriously, and they will *NOT* respect your attempts at becoming assertive. In some cases, I have seen where the perpetrating partner became more abusive toward the person making changes. Their anger can be a motivator for you to quit, or it can be a motivator for you to decide to stand tough and move forward. Of course, this will depend on how emotionally strong you are, and if you have been proactive in setting a plan for escape to safety.

When you get angry, do you usually say things you don't mean? Example: *"I'll quit this job if, or I'll leave you if, or I'll ground you for a year if, or I'll never speak to you again..."* If you set these kinds of boundaries and don't follow through, you'll lose the respect and credibility of those around you. If you are angry or frustrated, this is the time you need to utilize that important tool I mentioned earlier about picking your time, place, and rehearsal. Rehearse what you want to say and how you want to say it. This will enable you to deal more effectively with the pressures you are feeling.

Whatever happens, do not allow anyone to back you down, not even you. You'll find some people that say they care about you and love you, yet they use every tool at their disposal to control you and force you into backing down or quitting. They use things like bribery, fear, intimidation, and one very strong tool referred to as *Emotional Blackmail*.

EMOTIONAL BLACKMAIL

Emotional blackmail is when someone uses your negative history against you. They will rub your past in your face until you blow up, then they will move in to control you. Remember, you have the **right** to pick your time and place, and to rehearse what you want to say!

How do you defend your boundaries? Following are several things you can do to defend your boundaries:

1. When asking for what you want, be clear and direct. Keep it short, simple, and to the point. This tells others that you know what you want; it commands respect.

2. Take care of yourself, pamper yourself and protect your integrity. What is integrity? My personal definition is this… *"Integrity is a choice; it is constantly choosing the purity of truth, over popularity or desire and having the courage to follow through, regardless of the difficulties or consequences."* This is a difficult thing to get used to because it forces you to set and defend your boundaries and to take responsibility for your actions. It also demonstrates to others a command for respect. By pampering and nurturing yourself, you will learn to spot those things that are hurtful, abusive, or invasive. This allows you an opportunity to react appropriately and get it fixed.

3. *"Respect Others' Reality!"* Be objective about the behavior of others toward you. Respecting someone's reality is difficult to get used to. If you respect one's reality, it doesn't mean you have to like it, agree with it, or even accept it. It simply means that you'll allow others to have their own opinions, just as you want others

to respect yours. Respecting one's reality has no effect on you, whatsoever. You have a right to your own beliefs as do they, so give them the same respect you desire. I have a philosophy about life, situations, and people... *"If I don't like a movie, I get up and leave."* Respecting one's reality should be a boundary of yours.

4. In defending your boundaries you need to ascertain what your bottom line will be. Ask yourself, "how many times will I allow others to violate my boundaries?" In some circumstances, you may want to be flexible; however, in others you may need to adopt a no tolerance attitude. You are in control of your life and your boundaries... No one else is! Part of changing your behaviors is learning to put your trust in yourself, rather than placing your trust in others. You do this by having a good support group, someone that wants you to succeed as much as you do. Many times this may be your children, or it could be your higher power... So, do it for them, as well as for yourself. What's most important is that you don't allow yourself to be controlled by others. You also should not expect perfection from yourself. Accept and understand that you are a fallible human being, just like everyone else. It is OKAY to make mistakes, so long as you learn from them!

Concerning choices, sometimes we are fearful of making a choice or making a decision, and occasionally we simply don't know how. The problem arises when, by not making a choice, you've automatically made the decision to let things remain the way they are. Also, when looking at changing behaviors or lifestyles, by NOT making a decision to change, you have chosen to remain status quo. And, if the status quo is abusive, you have nothing to complain about!

ACCOUNTABILITY AND RESPONSIBILITY

Accountability and responsibility are a subject many people interject their own interpretation to and never look any further. When using accountability and responsibility, it is important to look at the whole picture and consider other noteworthy terms that go with it to clarify the true meaning and existence.

Take the bible, for example… some people accept only those things that make them feel good and ignore other areas that might inhibit their lifestyles. I believe this to be selective learning. When considering changing behaviors, I believe these concepts are crucial.

I have worked with many addicts and perpetrators of domestic violence, most of them admit they have a problem taking responsibility. When asked what they are going to do to fix it *(accept accountability)*, they become defensive and begin pointing fingers and placing blame on others for their actions, behaviors, and decisions. This behavior is not limited to addicts and domestic violence perpetrators; this is a huge part of *non-assertive* behavior. This is not limited to one group of people; it covers all ages, genders, ethnicities, and educational levels. These attitudes don't make their behaviors right; in fact, it makes things much worse.

Consider addicts and how society and loved ones, although well intended, enable the behavior of addicts by offering free amenities (or at very low cost) and then do not hold them responsible or accountable for their actions. I am not saying this modality is completely wrong. However, if society would create a centrally based structure that holds these people totally accountable for their own actions and behaviors, they would have a better success rate. This program should incorporate an emotional support system combined with excellent therapeutic programs based on Cognitive Behavioral, Rational Emotive, and Reality therapies to deal with personal needs and issues on an individual and group basis.

We send horribly mixed messages when we enable these people, and then when we see them on the street, we curse them and do our best to segregate them. This is a bit hypocritical, don't you think?

I see a huge need to have classes in schools that teach problem solving, anger management, assertiveness, self-empowerment, and others, instead of repeating the same old techniques that have little or no success. I find it wrong to clump these individuals arbitrarily into groups just because of some commonality, such as alcohol or drug addiction. I hear the excuse that it would cost too much or there's not enough interest. When you look at what our society is paying to correct the problems created from bad behaviors, there is no comparison. What price do you put on your life and your future?

Self-empowerment and assertiveness are the right way to go. Otherwise, we continue to enable the bad behavior. Even though this is a different issue to be discussed at a later time, the rules for change and for creating a healthy lifestyle are the same.

Looking further into the meaning of responsibility and accountability, there has to be a full commitment. This commitment has to be with us, and with the *issue* of acceptance of responsibility and accountability being addressed.

You must commit to yourself that you are going to follow through with whatever is to be done. This is what I refer to as, *Emotional Integrity."* Emotional integrity is simply saying what you mean, meaning what you say, and having the courage (commitment) to follow through, regardless of the difficulties involved! This is difficult to do at times, but the rewards are great. You will attain so many personal and intimate rewards, as well as the rewards gained from others around you. You will also give your children a wonderful gift, as well as provide a positive influence for others to follow. Consider this when writing the legacy you want to create for yourself.

How long are you willing to be a victim by not taking responsibility and accountability for your own personal actions and behaviors? Your progress is stagnated by not accepting this responsibility and accountability... Is it not?

Each of us has the right to choose whether we want to change or not. Using excuses such as, *"This is hard..., I can't do it..., I'm afraid..., I'll lose him or her..., They won't like me anymore..., I had to do it..., It was their fault..., I was told to do it..., He made me do it...,"* are all justifications that allow you to place blame on someone else. We passionately avoid taking and accepting our own personal responsibility and accountability.

To change behaviors, we need to change our thoughts, thought processes, and our perceptions. Remember, you are the only one in control of your choices, decisions, and behaviors. You have to believe that you are *NOT* helpless. Helplessness is not necessarily giving up our control; helplessness comes from what you do *not* say or do!

Accepting responsibility and accountability is one of the most important hurdles you might go through in accomplishing your goals for assertiveness and emotional freedom. Anything worth having does not come easy. When we work hard and experience those difficulties associated with change, we will respect and embrace it more… It will become ours!

Ladies and gentlemen, there are only two things in our lives that no one individual, group or organization can take away from us. People can take your money, your life, and your property, they can even take your family. However, they cannot take your integrity or your dignity. We already know what integrity means, but what about *dignity*? Simply put, dignity is the honesty you possess for yourself and for others around you. It is how you and others perceive yourself. Here again, this is a choice. You can choose to live your life with integrity and dignity or not. They go hand-in-hand; you can't have one without the other.

Note: One of the most difficult things for me to do in facilitating change was to identify my actions and why I did some of the things I did. My actions were usually bad, and like many people, it was easier to blame others for my bad behavior. It was very difficult to accept the responsibility and accountability for my own behaviors; to make a hard and fast commitment to change them was frightening. It was equally difficult to identify and believe that my personal rights were real, and that I had a choice whether I was going to own them or not.

People who tell you to *"just put things behind you, or forget about what happened"* are really telling you to bury your head in the sand and hope the problems will go away without any effort. Problems never simply go away; they have to be dealt with in a personal confrontation, most of which is done internally within you. It wasn't easy for me or any of my clients, but success is out there. The question is truly how seriously do you want emotional freedom and personal independence and what are you willing to do to get it?

I find when speaking with people, they have a tendency to take the long way around before getting to the subject, and sometimes, they rarely get there. They just go on, and on, and on, never getting to the point. I am sure you have experienced this. I love my wife, but when we first met, she did this often. The reason why people do this is because they want to make sure that **you,** as the listener, hear everything. Conversely, it is more effective for you to get to the point. If the listener needs more information, they will ask questions. Getting right to the point is more effective than other forms of conversation and is the main purpose of the Bonsai Principle. It reduces arguments and defuses tempers. I have used this format for years in my marriage, as well as with other relationships; it is most effective and much less frustrating.

YOU CAN CHANGE YOUR LIFE
BY CHANGING YOUR HEART.

*"Once we believe in ourselves,
we can risk curiosity, wonder, spontaneous delight,
or any experience that reveals the human spirit."*

~ e.e. cummings~

CHAPTER **5**

How Do You Change?

"Assertiveness is what we DO…it's NOT who we are!"

"Change" is a term that has a wide range of meanings and instills many different feelings and emotions; let's examine it. Change, according to the Webster's Dictionary (1993), is *to make a difference; to alter or to modify; the will; to make over radically; to transform, convert. These definitions infuse fear, hesitation, insecurity, and personal doubt, etc.* It infers another fear instilling term, *"commitment."* In order to facilitate a successful change it is prudent to make a commitment to that process. The mere idea of making a commitment is frightening to some. One should possess a will, a desire to change. That will be difficult if there was no commitment to yourself or to the act of change.

If we keep it simple, change is nothing more than making a commitment to take a risk. If we commit to change to become assertive, we gain a set of skills that will enable our lives to improve. Remember that when we begin this process, we will experience opposition from all sides, usually from family and friends. Do not let this opposition force you to quit! People will use all forms of trickery, deception, emotional blackmail, guilt or shame in order to win you back. In order for us to successfully commit to this change into being assertive, consider the following and write down your answers to these steps.

1. First, it is important to examine and analyze the reasons why you need to make this change. Take the time to write down the pros and cons about why you need this change. Keep in mind the differences between the words, **"need"** and **"want."** I want a Mercedes Benz; however, I don't *need* one! Be open-minded; use your heart to guide you, not your head. Remember the definition of integrity and use it. This examination will identify the purpose of our commitment.

2. It is important we give ourselves permission to make that commitment, and then to give ourselves permission to make mistakes in the process. We will make mistakes…and it is absolutely okay!! Instead of worrying about making a mistake, we should reframe it to be, *"when I make a mistake, what can I learn from it?"*

3. We previously discussed self-therapy and self-talk. We all do this from time to time, whether we realize it or not. Most people do this incorrectly and with improper information. This is where a positive outlook and *"rehearsal"* comes in. To do this, find a place where you can be alone to think about what you need to say to support your new agenda. When you have that figured out then you need to rehearse *aloud* what you want to say and how you need to say it. Feel what you are saying as you say it; use inflection when necessary to make your point. How does this make you feel to hear your own words? What affect does it have on you? In this particular scenario, you might want to say to yourself, *"no matter what, I give myself permission to commit to this important life change and become assertive to improve my life. I give myself permission to make as many mistakes as necessary to achieve my goal of assertiveness, because it is okay to make those mistakes. I commit 100% to practice assertiveness to improve my life."* Say it aloud with passion and conviction. It has to be formulated in a very positive manner, without doubt, hesitation, or reservation. In the beginning you may need to do self-talk a couple of times each day; once in the morning and then again before going to bed. Go into the bathroom where you have a bit of privacy. The next step

is very important... Look yourself in the eyes, focus on your eyes, and then rehearse aloud. You will feel a bit odd or even silly, but do not let that prevent you from completing this exercise. If this is simply too uncomfortable, take the time while you are on a walk, or whenever you are alone, and rehearse aloud. Do this every time you begin to feel unsure or shaky in your commitment, or when obstacles arise that stifle your attempts. You can do this self-talk in every situation, and I highly advise you to follow through.

4. **Confrontation** is a situation where rehearsal works extremely well. Use it... It works! Confrontation is a misunderstood concept that will be discussed in more detail later in the book. Let's set some guidelines that will help you begin the process. Always remember to pick your time, place... and then rehearse.

Guidelines to help you rehearse

1. After figuring out the message you want to relay, say it aloud. Feel and hear the words and the tone you choose so that you are saying it the way you intend. The selection of words is as important as the tone used.

2. Be cognizant of the physical aspects of an assertive person and then mimic them. Be aware of your posture, eye contact, and your confidence. Keep in mind that more than 93 percent of effective communication is non-verbal; it is body language, both yours and theirs.

3. Every time you are engage in a difficult or stressful situation, your avoidance behaviors are set in motion. It is important for you to control them.

4. While you are in the act of self-talk, utilize the concept of time, place, and rehearsal, and use your relaxation techniques. This is an excellent defense for difficult and stressful situations.

5. It is vitally important that you remain calm and become comfortable in any situation you may encounter. This is not always possible,

but with practice, we can be successful in almost every situation. Remember, being assertive is what you do... It's a lifestyle; it is not who you are. It is sometimes difficult to be assertive when it is really necessary to do so. When using assertiveness daily, it does become a lifestyle, so it will be there when you need it. Remember, you will run the gamut of personality types from time to time; this is normal.

6. Let's look at **"timing."** What does timing really mean? When we are confronted with a situation and are caught off guard, this is when you need to choose *"your"* time and place. For example, you might say to the other individual, *"let's talk later,"* or *"I'll call you back in a few minutes,"* or *"let me think about it."* Making some kind of statement that will afford you some time to think and rehearse an appropriate response. This will ensure that you have time to offer a suitable and assertive response. Something as simple as *pausing* before responding, will give you a bit of time, as well. This will draw the respect you deserve from others because you are giving both yourself and the other person time to reflect without pressure.

7. Keep a **"Cool Head"** about yourself. When people are angry, they are the most vulnerable to being controlled and manipulated. By keeping a cool head, you increase your anger management, thought processes, and problem solving skills. This will also attract respect from others.

8. Because 93 to 95 percent of all communications is non-verbal *(body language and facial expressions),* it is important to be very aware of the other persons physical reaction to what you are saying and doing, especially if this person is volatile?

9. If you know you are going to be confronted, or you are going to have to confront someone else, there are three things that may help. Exercise, deep breathing, and putting a physical and comfortable distance between you and the other person will ease the situation a bit.

It's important to remember that you do not control anyone or anything; you can only control yourself, and how people and situations affect you. It is not the traumatic or stressful situations that define us …it is how we DEAL with those difficult times that defines who you are!

Effective communication is getting your point across without being offensive or aggressive. It's also a form of communication to get what you *NEED*, not what you want**!!**

10. Use the Bonsai Principle. Always keep it short, simple, and to the point. Leave the rest of the useless dialogue out. This is difficult to accomplish, at times. Passive, passive-aggressive, and even aggressive personality types have a bad habit of going all the way around a subject before they get to the point, and sometimes they never do. By maintaining the Bonsai Principle, it does several things. It assists us in getting our point across with little or no confusion, and it reduces stress, anxiety, and anger. It will ultimately cause us to gain respect from our peers, and our self-esteem, self-respect, and confidence will vastly increase. Would you not agree that this is a wonderful concept? We should all remember that this takes work, determination, desire, and personal commitment.

11. Always, always concentrate on the issue, and **NOT** on the person. At all costs, avoid making *"you"* statements. This will keep the conversation from getting personal and reduce further complications. In other words, *"you did this or that, you said this or that, etc."* We'll review this more in depth later in the book. Refrain from asking *"why"* questions, such as *"why did you do that?"* Be cautious using *"when"* questions as these can be viewed in the same way as *"why"* questions, creating defensiveness in the person with whom you are communicating.

12. You need to remember that you, and you alone are responsible for your behavior and actions. This is what being assertive means. It also means, that you are responsible for being aware

and considerate of the feelings and personal rights of others, as well as your own and that of your families.

13. Utilize *"Humor."* This is a wonderful and effective way of de-escalating anger, anxiety, and stress. Although with strangers, humor may do the opposite and exacerbate the problem. Do not use *"Self-Belittling"* humor; allow yourself the respect you deserve. Many times, humor may intensify the problem with one who is already angry, so you might consider another avenue. Be aware of hidden aggression; often you can see this in the body language, facial expressions, and vocal tones of the other person.

14. Find yourself a mentor with someone you respect and mimic those characteristics you most admire. Keep in mind the feelings and personal rights of others and practice, practice, practice. Ask yourself how your mentor would respond to this situation?

15. Be aware of your personal safety, such as with a violent spouse or someone that is experiencing heightened anger. Ask yourself if it is safe to be in this situation! Is it safe for you to be assertive at this time? Should you pick another time and place?

Note: It is well-known that children are very resilient. In almost every circumstance they are placed in, children have the inherent ability to adapt. The older they are; however, the less likely this wonderful characteristic will remain with them. If you make a concerted effort to absorb these tools and techniques and take these concepts to heart, you'll be on your way to regaining some resiliency.

Being resilient is being willing to conform, being flexible with your boundaries, and embracing change. This does not mean you have to kiss any rump, or do things that you don't feel comfortable doing. It means that you have a choice in your decisions; you are in total control of your life. This should allow you to regain your resiliency. When approached and perceived correctly, change can be a wonderfully exciting journey.

"*No man or woman is worth your tears,
and the one who is, won't make you cry.*"

~Author Unknown·~

CHAPTER **6**

Non-Verbal Communication

Non-Verbal Assertiveness

Neurolinguistics state that approximately 55% of communication is physiological, which is the physical and chemical functions and actions of our bodies. Roughly 35% is tonality and 7% is verbal. Which supports the premise that 5 to 8% of our communication is verbal.

What is it like to act assertively? Remember, the greatest part of effective communication is *"nonverbal,"* which is our body language. We are going to explore what non-verbal assertiveness looks like. Let's first look at the passive and passive-aggressive postures. As discussed previously, we cannot control anyone but ourselves. However, we must remember that we have a huge responsibility in how we influence others! We influence people, whether we intend to do so or not. Our body language is the first impression that will make or break us.

With passive and passive-aggressive behaviors, these individuals do their best to become invisible. They don't feel comfortable or confident enough to be noticed. Being invisible makes their life much easier to cope with, and they don't have to worry as much, allegedly resulting in lower stress levels. In reality, their stress levels actually increase because they are so focused on not being seen.

Are you aware that we teach people how to treat us? This teaching process begins with the first impression you give to other people. Your body language is how they get their first impression of you. It is what they see in you, just as what you see in them that creates this first impression. It could be said that your body language is your advertising; therefore, wouldn't it be prudent to be assertive?

Have you ever simply looked at someone and thought to yourself that this person is aggressive, or you don't trust them, or wow, this person looks like someone you'd like to get to know? It is because of their advertising. When you met your spouse or significant other, what did you tell yourself about them? What did you think? This was your first impression of them, and because it was favorable you continued forward to having a relationship. It was their advertising that caused this reaction in you.

ASSERTIVE POSTURE

What makes up our non-verbal communication? It begins with our posture. Examine how you stand and walk; assertive people stand and walk erect, NOT slumped, slouched, or bent over. It's standing erect with your head high; your back is straight and you are NOT looking down at the floor. A proper standing distance from someone is 1 to 3 feet away. With our peripheral vision, we should be able to see the other persons feet. If we can't, it's because we are too close, and we may be invading their space. Assertive posture is looking straightforward and making appropriate eye contact to the person with whom we are communicating. Don't glare or stare, and it's okay to blink.

Walk and stand with a feeling of inner confidence and peace, as though you like and respect yourself. What this means is that your hair is combed, teeth brushed, face washed, and your clothes are neat and clean. This will project to others that you have self-respect, confidence, and are assertive. It shows that you are approachable and likeable.

It is good to smile and also very important to *"feel"* the smiles that come your way. Smiling and nodding are forms of greetings and are considered friendly gestures. This behavior doesn't cost you a thing, but will come back to you ten-fold. Now you are beginning to teach people how to treat you, non-verbally. This is just the first step in being assertive. The difficult part is when you verbally communicate with someone.

In general conversation you will see opportunities to speak your boundaries, i.e. your likes and dislikes. Pay attention to body language; it tells you volumes about how you are affecting the other person. Listen to the words others use in response to you. It will also tell you volumes about what they are actually saying and if they are truly interested in you or are just being polite.

Pay attention to how the new relationship is coming along and be aware of the differences between the old and the new. You'll be pleasantly surprised how respectful people treat you; this in itself is addicting.

Those with passive and passive-aggressive behaviors many times become leery of others. When someone smiles at them, they sometimes wonder what it is they want, instead of accepting it as a friendly gesture. *Trust begins within you, the individual!* You will need to trust yourself first! Again, we cannot give something to anyone else if we don't possess it ourselves. When we have been hurt, cheated on, lied to, used, and physically and emotionally abused, we will not allow ourselves to trust anyone, making it that much more difficult to trust ourselves. We begin to mistrust our own judgment. Does this behavior work for you? Does it make you happy? Are your relationships going well? Do you trust yourself or is it others you don't trust? This is the time you seriously need to look deep inside yourselves and determine if you actually do trust yourself. If not, why, and what is it that's going to motivate us to change?

It has been my experience that people who have suffered certain types of injustices, lose the ability, confidence, and self-esteem to trust themselves. They believe they have made so many bad decisions in their life that they will continue to make them. It is important to understand that it is okay to make mistakes as long as we learn from them. Learn the tools in this book and practice them daily to learn how not to make bad decisions; this will help you learn to trust yourself again. It is important to understand that we are *NOT* perfect; we are fallible. Therefore, we will make mistakes...and it's okay. Learn what to do and what not to do for the next time. Does the fear of trust get you what you need? It doesn't! This is why it is important to become assertive, to believe and trust in yourself and your own judgment, and to accept the reality that you are not now, nor will you ever be, perfect. You will make mistakes. Look at it this way, if you're *NOT* making mistakes, you're *NOT* doing anything to progress, and you are *NOT* putting your reciprocal boundaries in place and defending them. You are not allowing yourself to be free and happy.

If you want to feel good about yourself, take it to the next level and offer a nice compliment to some of those people in the service industry, such as waitresses, clerks, and custodians. By simply telling someone you appreciate their efforts and recognize that they are really busy is huge to them. They will appreciate it and it will come back to you almost immediately. The feelings you receive from your accomplishments will make you feel very good inside, and it makes others feel good, as well. The more confident you become, the more people will respond to you in a positive way. Let me repeat this... The more confident **you** become, the more people will respond to you in a positive way.

I have noticed when I am depressed or frustrated, if I force myself to give these kinds of compliments to people, I begin to lose the depression or frustration and become more positive and assertive. Yes, I do get depressed and frustrated at times, as does most everyone else.

MOVEMENTS

Your bodily movements will complement your posture. People move in a manner in which they feel. If you feel depressed, frustrated, angry, or even happy and excited, you are going to walk, talk, and gesture according to those feelings and emotions. This is why they call it, *"non-verbal communication,"* and this is what gives others their first impression of you.

These movements need to be positive, with an assertive tone. In other words, move with confidence, be self-assured, and present a friendly attitude. Make eye contact and use your hands in a non-aggressive manner. If you feel confident, your body movements, head movements, and hand gestures will move smoothly. People will feel at ease around you because they see that you are at ease with yourself.

VOCAL TONES

Tones are made by the stretching and tension placed on the vocal chords. This creates the pitch of sounds emitted from your mouth when you speak, which affect your feelings and emotions. Tones are equally as important as your bodily movements. In some cases, your vocal tones point out your personality type.

Passive and passive-aggressive people talk very softly because they most generally do not like being heard. They prefer to be invisible, so they sometimes mumble or stutter. Many times passive and passive-aggressive people don't enunciate their words. We can detect fear, a lack of confidence, a low self-esteem, and nervousness in their tones. If we think about it, we sometimes make judgments about people by hearing their vocal tones.

An aggressive person's tone is usually loud, obnoxious, belittling, offensive, intimidating, and/or threatening. They use these tones because of a lack of self-esteem, and they are fearful of being found out. They are hiding something, or they need to have a feeling of control; they are angry for whatever reason. Aggressive people feel they need to be that way to get anything done or to get what they want. The result is they are not happy. They push people away, they destroy relationships, and many times they lose their jobs.

Assertive people speak with confidence and a positive attitude that respects the rights and boundaries of others. They will sound warm, relaxed, and well modulated. They have an even flow, and it is confident and inviting. In conversation, it is easy to assess one's emotional state, how they feel about the issues being discussed, or about the person involved in the discussion.

FACIAL EXPRESSIONS

Facial expressions are influenced, as well by how we feel, which stems from our personality type. Your facial expressions are the very first point of contact we have with another person. Passive and passive-aggressive people display an expression that denotes sadness, emptiness, a lack of confidence and a low self-esteem, etc. They usually sport a blank or sad look.

Aggressive people usually have a scowl on their face, a look of anger to warn people off that they don't want to be approached. At times, they sport a distant look, as if they are not sure of what is going on around them.

Assertive people are perceived approachable, friendly, open, trusting, kind, respectful, etc., which sounds very similar to the motto of the girl scouts or boy scouts; they have many of the same qualities.

Non-verbal communication from an assertive person emanates self-respect and respect for others. It also demonstrates that our point of view will be heard. Therefore, if we incorporate an assertive posture, vocal tones, and facial expressions, our first and last impressions will be easily and positively influenced.

HELPFUL GUIDELINES FOR BEING ASSERTIVE

1. When interacting with people, relax before you begin and then stay relaxed. To help stress subside, take in deep breaths through your nose and slowly blow it out through your mouth. Do this several times.
2. *Rehearse* what you want to say and how you want to say it. Rehearsing helps us be more confident about the subject. Give yourself permission to make mistakes.
3. Respect the reality of others. Show an openness and willingness to listen. We don't have to like it, accept it, or agree with it, but we do need to recognize and respect it.
4. It is imperative that we have *Emotional Integrity*. We should say what we mean, mean what we say and have the courage (commitment) to follow through.
5. You don't have to apologize for your opinions as long as you don't criticize others for theirs. This is respecting their reality. Accept that you don't know it all, and that you are fallible.
6. Don't threaten or intimidate anyone.
7. Don't allow yourself to be threatened by others.
8. Don't let things slide, take care of them immediately so you feel complete and successful.
9. Acknowledge your successes and your downfalls so you continue to grow in a positive way.
10. Be cognizant and respectful of the feelings and emotions of others. Watch their body language to see how you are affecting them.

DO NOT GIVE UP…BE PROUD AND EXCITED ABOUT YOURSELF AND YOUR NEW LIFESTYLE!!!

Note: This form of communication is wonderful if you are able to become proficient at it. I was in state and federal law enforcement before I became a therapist, and I use the same techniques of observing body language to assist me in helping people. As a law enforcement officer, the guidelines for effective communication helped me to determine if someone was not being truthful with me.

In therapy, it not only helps to determine if someone is deceitful, it also helps me determine their fears. It allows me to see if I am hitting a nerve, if I am on track. Understanding body language will help in all relationships and is a huge asset if you can learn to read it. The whole concept of non-verbal communication is extremely valuable.

FORGIVENESS

Forgiveness is a horribly misunderstood concept. It has caused people to become angry, fearful, frustrated, selfish, resentful, and has even given some people an excuse to isolate and hide. Here again, we need to have a clear understanding of what forgiveness is, who it is ultimately for, and what it will do for us.

Many people experience trouble with this concept. Victims of all forms of abuse and addicts seem to have the most difficulty. The dictionary defines forgiveness as..."*To cease resentments against, to grant relief from, or to give up resentment.*"

Forgiveness, to the majority of people, denotes the opposite of what it really means. The reason people become angry, fearful, frustrated, selfish, or resentful is because they feel if they forgive the person who hurt them, it means that what happened to them was okay. Believe me when I tell you, this is as far from the truth as you can get. It is a horrible misunderstanding, because what happened to you is NOT okay, and it never will be!

Question: Why would you want to forgive someone who has hurt you or victimized you, someone who demonstrated deliberate disrespect for you? Do you believe it would help this other person if you forgave them? Do you think they would respect you, care for you, even worry about you? Since they possess a non-caring attitude for you in the first place, they don't respect you or your safety. Do you think that forgiving this person would change their minds and attitude toward you? At best, they might apologize to you, but will they mean it?

Forgiveness is strictly for you and you alone! As is everything else in life, forgiveness is a choice; YOUR CHOICE! Forgiving is what you do for *yourself*, not something you do for others.

When you forgive, you give yourself *"permission"* to eliminate all the anger, fear, frustration, selfishness, and resentment that you hold inside of you. You cut yourself free of those feelings that continue to cause you grief in your life, so that you can move forward. By making a commitment to forgive those who have hurt you, you allow yourself to move forward; you give yourself a new start. Let me say this again, when you forgive the person who hurt you, you are *NOT* telling anyone this hurtful act was okay, it wasn't!!!! In fact, you don't have to tell the perpetrator or anyone else for that matter. However, it may become obvious by your actions and behavior. Your act of forgiveness for someone who has hurt you is between you and God, no one else.

If you examine the definition of forgiveness, it says that you will cease the feeling of resentment against the other person. Again, this is a choice; your choice. It means that you are going to grant yourself relief from that hurt. You are going to give up the resentment you feel deep in your heart, so that you are able to move forward!

The pain of what happened to you is inevitable, you can't stop it. However, the decision to continue suffering is yours. If you need to, please review the previous section on fear. Fear prevents people from forgiving. People who have been victimized all too often pick up where the perpetrator left off. The victim begins to validate and believe the abuse and cognitive distortions that have been given to them. An example of this is that they may believe they deserve the abuse and are not worth anything better. No one has the right to abuse you…just as you do not have the right to abuse anyone else or yourself! This is a powerful tool that needs to be committed to, believed in, and utilized.

What's worse than suffering from past abuse is living with the constant reminders and thoughts of that abuse even **one day** longer than you have to, because it is almost as painful as the original hurt. Make the decision NOT to cling to those negative, destructive feelings. Anger is nothing more than an outward expression of the hurt, fear, grief, and frustration you live with. Even though the memory may never disappear completely, forgiving the perpetrator will release you from the emotional pain and reduce those negative, hurtful feelings.

There isn't a specific timeline, schedule, or itinerary for choosing to forgive that you need to follow. For some people, forgiveness is spontaneous. For others, it may take weeks, months, or even years, and with great effort. Don't allow yourself to take years for forgiveness to transpire. Taking years is a lot of wasted time out of your life. Do not allow the perpetrator to take anymore of your life than they already have.

Keep in mind that you cannot change what has happened to you. If you accept the fact that you alone have the ability to control how you will interpret and respond to these events, you'll be stronger and more in control of your future. If you willingly accept this responsibility, you will succeed.

We talked about self-talk and self-therapy earlier in this book. This is when positive self-talk is important. You need to listen to the messages you tell yourself. I recommend that you write them down and do not censor them. Go back later when you are relaxed and calm with a clear head and review them. After reviewing them, ask yourself if you are being fair and honest with yourself? Should you make changes, and if so, where? If you find you are not being fair or honest, then reframe them until you are.

One important step in your growth is to share your experience with others. Find the person or persons that support you in your growth and share your experiences with them. As a suggestion, you might consider using God, or whatever your higher power might be. Several things will take place if you do. You'll find that you are not the only person who has experienced painful events, that there are some people who have experienced similar or worse things in their lives, and you'll create new relationships. In sharing with others, you will hear what others are saying and feeling, which will give you a different perspective. You may likely find solutions to your suffering and allow yourself to do an emotional checkup. Don't be the kind of person that puts themselves in a relationship where they might be thriving in one area and suffering a great deal in another. Example: A woman may care deeply about a man who doesn't show her the same affection. She becomes "stuck" in the belief that he will change. The problem escalates when she begins to believe distorted thoughts that she is not doing all that is necessary for that change to occur. She doesn't realize the change she seeks is not her decision to make, it is his. She can not control him or his decisions.

"*Seek first to understand then to be understood.*"

~Author Unknown~

CHAPTER **7**

Being Present

Have you ever heard the saying, *"you need to stand up and be counted?"* That is essentially what it means to be *"present."* You have to be there in the moment, physically and emotionally. Many times this can be difficult to do, but with practice and determination, you can conquer this feat. Let's begin by examining our physical presence.

Physical Presence:

Our physical presence needs to be assertive. Our posture, bodily movements, and facial expressions are the characteristics that cause others to develop their first impression of us. Therefore, it is vitally important to consider rehearsing these for our comfort and confidence.

GIVING YOUR OPINION

In order for you to be heard, respected, communicated with, loved, admired, wanted and needed, and in order for your needs to be met, you must be present, in the moment, so-to-speak. You *NEED* to be seen! You must speak up to be heard. People need to know that you exist emotionally, as well as physically.

Question: How do you become present in your own life?

As a Passive or Passive-Aggressive person, it is important to be present to achieve what we need; sometimes this is difficult to overcome, but *NOT* impossible. As an assertive person, we actively participate in all events of our life! We need to begin making our own decisions. It is important for us to accept responsibility for our actions and our life, and it is okay to ask for advice. Understand that when you ask for advice, it is the practice of sharing ideas, thoughts, suggestions, opinions, goals, likes, dislikes, aspirations, and dreams. Once you have done that, then you make up your mind with logic and education. There are no rules requiring us to accept that advice. It is your right to reject it.

Be open and honest and express your opinions. These are your feelings and emotions, your likes and dislikes, as well as your displeasures. Displeasures are those things or situations that cause you emotional and or physical discomfort, those things that contradict *your* lifestyle. By following these steps, and setting and defending your reciprocal boundaries, you are creating your emotional body armor.

What or who in your life prevents you from being assertive? Write these down, analyze them. Examine the pros and cons and the advantages versus the disadvantages. In doing this, you will be in a better position to make educated decisions. Understand why these things are stopping you, formulate a plan to change them and then make a commitment to follow through. Practice emotional integrity; say what you mean, mean what you say, and have the courage (commitment) to follow through, regardless of the difficulties or consequences you might encounter. By doing this, you have increased your opportunities for success tremendously. You are also setting your boundaries and teaching people how to respect you.

EMPATHIC LISTENING/ACTIVE LISTENING

It has been my experience that empathic listening or active listening is something most of society does not do. Active listening is a vital part of all relationships and a significant function for effective communication. Usually people listen only to what they want to hear and nothing more; this is selective listening and is brought about by one's experiences, desires, or how they are feeling at the time. Society moves at such a fast pace, people get tangled up in their own lives and problems, and sometimes listening becomes a very low priority. However, if you are self-aware and are cognizant of the particulars of your life experiences and put forth an honest effort, you can succeed at this concept. The bottom line is that most people do not actively listen.

The results of active listening are that we will not only fulfill the needs of others, but we also fulfill our own needs at the same time. Active listening demonstrates that you care about what the speakers are saying, and that you respect them and their issues. Isn't this what you desire in your life?

In order to be truly empathic, it is fundamentally essential for us to actively listen. During the process of stating your opinion, this tool is extremely important in building and maintaining relationships. Active listening is a process of concentrating on the speaker and *their* issues, *not* on yours. It allows you to learn and ultimately understand more about the person with whom you are communicating. Remember, if you want to be understood, first you need to understand!

Question: What is the difference between *empathy* and *sympathy*?

Empathy is having an understanding of someone else's situations or experiences based on our own personal experiences of similar events. It is having the ability to see things through someone's eyes and understand their particular experiences. This offers both you and the other person some common ground.

For example, if we had an opportunity to speak with a young soldier who fought in a war, and we had a conversation about death and how it affects people, could you both relate? Most people I have spoken with think not. I disagree. The emotional affects of experiencing the loss of a friend or loved one is very much the same, no matter when or how it happens. The feelings we experience from the death of someone are equal, regardless of the circumstances of how they died. It carries no less importance or severity, whether the loss was during a war or by natural causes. Death is the common factor that both parties can empathize about.

Sympathy is simply feeling sorry for someone. If you are truly concerned about another person, take your responsibility to heart and listen empathically. Listen to the words, feelings, and emotions of that person. Very importantly, watch the body language of how you are affecting that person. You will begin to see much more of this individual's make up than ever before and your relationship will grow to a more positive level.

Listening empathically is *"listening selflessly,"* while placing your own concerns aside to focus on the speaker and their issues. It looks something like this:

Listening → Understanding → Responding

Active *listening* leads to *understanding*, which leads us to *respond* more appropriately! All listening techniques, empathic and active, are NOT behaviors or a state of mind, they are a personal effort and commitment.

Listen accurately by asking for clarification when needed. Listen for the true meaning of what is being spoken and lastly, use empathy. In order for you to be completely attentive, you might have to turn off the radio or TV or you may have to leave the room. Whatever it takes, do it, and you will succeed.

PROCESSING WHAT YOU HEAR

The next step is to accurately process the information you've received. We have never been taught how to do this. Generally, people react without thinking. As a society, we have become a nation of reactors instead of being pro-actors.

The act of processing means we objectively analyze the information we receive and allow ourselves to formulate a logical conclusion. It is not just taking the verbal dialogue into consideration, although the verbal dialogue is a big part of this process. Processing information means considering everything from body language, facial expression, voice inflection and the words. Then put all this information into a mental pot and analyze it to form a conclusion. It requires getting a clear understanding of the speaker's intent. Here are some helpful tips for doing this... Identify key words, as well as the message and feelings being communicated. Ask yourself if what this person is saying coincides with their actions. If not, someone is not being honest. Consider clarifying the information for a clearer understanding. What is the real issue of this discussion? What is their intent? What exactly does this person want me to understand?

This is a very important concept and is useful in every relationship and conversation we take part in. The person's age is of no consequence. Ask open-ended questions... *"What do you think? What are your thoughts? Where did you get this information? How do you feel about...? When can I expect...? Can you explain what you mean by...? What are the consequences of...?"* Beginning your questions with, *"why"* will make the other person defensive and possibly angry, so take care not to use them. If you do, your conversations are at great risk of going negative. Beginning your questions with, *"What or How"* will always cause thought provoking responses.

Note: By using open-ended questions, I have found that people are more likely to come around to your way of thinking, especially if you ask enough questions. By forming your questions this way, it causes people to examine their own behaviors. It causes them to think about what they are saying and doing. It gives them a feeling of control over their own lives, which is a right that we all possess. It is giving them the feeling of respect and control over themselves.

Asking open-ended questions is both empowering and free. It can also be frightening if this individual has something to hide, or if they feel guilty or shameful. The process of asking open-ended questions is not intrusive or threatening. If you utilize the tools that have been presented thus far and apply the concept of forgiveness, you can become extremely insightful and influential with all the people in your life in a very appropriate and acceptable way. Regardless of what venue you are in, open ended questions are always useful and beneficial.

SELF-ACCEPTANCE

"Have patience with all things, but first with yourself. Never confuse your mistakes with your value as a human being.

You are a perfectly valuable, creative, worthwhile person simply because you exist, and no amount of triumphs, or tribulations can ever change that. Unconditional Self-acceptance is the core of a peaceful mind."

~Author Unknown~

CHAPTER **8**

U.S.A.

Unconditional Self-Acceptance

Unconditional Self-Acceptance (U.S.A.) is a wonderfully powerful concept. In order to achieve self-empowerment, it is vital to possess **U.S.A.** This is the most important step you will ever need to take. By attaining U.S.A., you are giving yourself permission to give and to acknowledge your personal value and importance in your world. It is important to develop tolerance and patience with everything and everyone; most importantly, with yourself, and then with others. It is essential not to confuse or measure your self-worth, your personal value, or importance as a human being by the mistakes you make or by the negative comments and opinions of others. The term unconditional means, *"without exception, unlimited, or unqualified."* When looking at ourselves and the life we are currently living, this is sometimes very difficult to do. Without limitations, what kind of person would we be?

In my case it was extremely difficult. This process forced me to examine my decisions, choices, and behaviors, as well as my thought processes, feelings, and emotions. It forced me to make the difficult decision to change or not. When I accepted responsibility and accountability for all of these things, without hesitation, I made a conscious choice to change! Believe me when I say it was the most difficult thing I ever did, but it has also been the most rewarding. I regained my identity and individuality!

Whether you have children or not, think about this for a moment... Would you stop loving your child if he/she came home with less than an acceptable report card, or if that child made mistakes more than other children? What if this child had an emotional disorder, or an unacceptable behavioral problem? Would you love them less or value them less because of those things? Would you give them away or disown them and no longer accept them? These are absurd questions, are they not? Of course you wouldn't stop loving them or disown them. With that in mind, can you accept yourself with the same fallibilities as they have? When I ask this question of my clients, many begin to rationalize and justify why they are not good enough to accept themselves. Doing that is a serious waste of time, energy, and growth and there is no logic that will support these rationalizations and justifications. If we can accept the fact that we are fallible human beings, we will spend much more of our time accepting ourselves and trying to improve on those imperfections. Since you have read this far, I have to assume you want to free yourself from years of negative feelings, thoughts, and beliefs. Therefore, it is my recommendation that you do something positive and not use rationalization and justification as your excuse to remain status quo.

It is important to understand that having U.S.A. means we must have a complete paradigm shift in how we see, think, and feel about all aspects of our lives, i.e. the past, present, and future. Stop seeing things through the eyes of others and value your own personal and individual attributes. Others have put thought distortions in our heads, and rationalizing causes us to pick up where they left off. It is important to learn to perceive things as they really are, through your eyes, with your God given intelligence and through your personal reality. It might be of great benefit to see yourself through God's eyes. The bottom line is this; everyone on this planet is imperfect and they make mistakes... it is okay and it is acceptable! Most of us are our own worst critics. We are harder on ourselves than anyone else is, and there is no reason to be. In neurolinguistics, it is estimated that approximately 77% of our core beliefs are negative, based on the general statistics. Therefore, don't you think this percentage would be much higher when you add those who experience low self-esteem, self-worth, and have little or no self-confidence? What about those who experience physical or emotional abuse? Moreover, if this hypothesis is true, can you see why it is imperative to have a paradigm shift?

When you are in the frame of mind of being your own worst enemy, it's easy to rationalize and justify our position and stay on the pity-pot. Doing this usually feels safe and natural, not necessarily happy or healthy, but safe. When this happens, ask yourself if this is working for you? Is it getting you what you need? Is it helping you develop that special relationship you have been dreaming about all your life? Are you becoming more successful in your career? If you are honest with yourself, it isn't working at all, is it? It is self-destructive to you and the people who care about you.

It is important to look at things from a positive perspective. For instance, when looking at a half-filled glass, do you see it as half-full or half empty? In utilizing self-therapy or self-talk, it states that you need to tell yourselves positive things to avoid the negative. The longer you are positive, the more your thoughts and behaviors will change toward the positive. You will become what you think and believe about yourself.

Look for the positive and utilize self-talk to support those thoughts and beliefs. Statements such as, *"that figures; it always happens to me, or why me"* are negative. By viewing things negatively, we put ourselves right back on the pity-pot of life, where we feel sorry for ourselves and place blame, point fingers, and reject responsibility for our own actions, behaviors, and choices.

Can you reframe the following statement to make it a positive? *"This is a bunch of b…s…. This pisses me off; it is not right!"* Why not say, *"Yes, this has happened, now what can I learn from it?"* What if you ask yourself, *"How can I change these thoughts or feelings?"* Would this make it a positive? Questions such as these will assist you in taking control of your life. They will assist you in finding a solution and will help create a boundary to reduce the possibility of it happening again.

Realize, understand, and accept the fact that bad things happen to good people! It is a fact of life, and it is normal. My purpose for saying this allows us to freely and openly accept the fact that, *"bad things do happen to good people"* and the only thing you can control about it is how it affects you. It happens to good people all the time and there is no way to avoid it. It is better and more productive to learn to deal with it in a positive fashion so you are enabled to learn from it! The trick to being happy most of the time is to find a way that allows you to learn something positive from the negative things that happen in your life. U.S.A. is really a very powerful concept and it does work, if you accept yourself and others as fallible human beings, without any expectations. Further, doing this will create a world of happiness and contentment.

Do not allow your fear, anger, frustration, anxiety, or depression to control the good common sensibilities you possess! Recognize and accept that *YOU ARE A "GOOD" PERSON*. At one time in your life you felt that and possibly believed it until you were convinced otherwise by those that are supposed to love you. It is also a fact of reality, and it is acceptable to get upset or even angry when bad situations happen to you. However, it is important to control your anger enough so it does not control you and cause you to hurt yourself or someone else. Yelling and screaming is how many of us release frustration that has built up inside of us, causing many of us to explode and lose control. If you have to yell and scream, try doing it in a pillow where others are not likely to hear.

Do you realize that when bad things happen to you, it is part of your learning curve? You can actually learn from these terrible things. Do you believe this is true? We are taught how to treat people, and we teach people how to treat us. Do you agree with that? You learned how to be angry, hateful, hurtful, and you have learned to dislike yourself! Is this the type of behavior and belief you want to pass down to your children or continue to live with? If you object to this, learn how to love and accept yourself for who and what you really are. Believe me when I tell you that you are a creative, valuable, and worthwhile person. I know this because of one very important reason; I personally believe God would never create anything that could be considered a waste of time!

There is no amount of success or triumph, and no amount of trials and tribulations that can ever change your values. Conversely, we are the only one that can devalue ourselves, and yet again, this is our decision. So please take care of yourself and love yourself.

UNCONDITIONAL SELF-ACCEPTANCE IS YOUR FOUNDATION TO A HAPPY AND HEALTHY LIFE!

With some effort and commitment and through the information, concepts, tools, and techniques in this book, we can achieve anything we choose to do, if we put our heart and mind to it! Find that motivating factor that will push you toward your success and enable you to make that all important commitment.

Note: For me, this was a very difficult concept to accept and change, because I had such a long running history of negative thoughts and beliefs. It was only when I met my wife that she demonstrated to me that I was worthy. She showed me I was a good man, that I was equal to everyone else, and that I had something special to offer others. I eventually realized it was up to me to accept this information as my own, or her meaningful observations would have been in vain.

When you give respect and consideration where it's due, you will earn respect in return, which has to begin in your heart. You are a valuable person. As I grew up, I was taught to believe that

I was worthless and no one would want me. I always had a distant hope in my heart that there was a better life somewhere. I was right… There was a better life for me. However, I did everything in my power to avoid the work and commitment necessary to achieve that life. I avoided all the right things because they were hard, sometimes painful, and they required change. They required a commitment from me, which made me more fearful. Even today, there are times when some of those negative beliefs still raise their ugly head and make me feel less than worthy, and I have to work diligently to dispel them.

I always blamed my folks and others around me. This is not to say my parents didn't have a great deal of negative influence, because they did. It came down to where I had to make a choice; did I want to die a miserable, lonely person, or did I want to be happy like many of the people I knew at that time? I had to make a commitment to do the work and go through the hurtful events I so faithfully avoided. I had to make a steadfast commitment not to quit. These were some very difficult times, and along the way I truly believed I would never make it. Oftentimes I wanted to quit; but, I didn't, and I am very happy for that decision.

I'd like to tell you a story of a man who led a pretty terrible life. He was a drunk and an adulterer. He was also physically and emotionally abusive to people. One day he ran into a life-threatening situation and he was dying. He made a promise to God and said, *"God, if you would allow me to live, I'll turn my life around and make a better world."* God allowed him to live. For several years, he did his best to honor his promise, but finally realized his efforts were futile. His frustration and anger grew day-by-day. One afternoon he found himself to be very angry and ran into the woods and fell to his knees. He began sobbing, yelling, screaming, and even cursing at God. He said, *"I have tried my best, and I can't make a better world…I just can't! I am nothing more than a mere mortal…I can't make the world better."* Suddenly his head fell to the ground and God said to him, *"My son, you are just a man. But, you can make a better world, simply by making a better you."* Although this is just a story, it has much truth in its meaning. When you make a better you, you possess a very powerful tool that enables you to influence the world and people around you to become better. Embrace U.S.A. and your personal value and you will begin to make your world better because you are making a better you. I cannot stress enough that this is a difficult thing to do, however, you can be a success as long as you commit to yourself and to the task on a day-to-day basis.

*Always keep in mind those who show
you encouragement when you are down."*

~Author Unknown~

CHAPTER 9

Feedback

"Give the gift of healthy relationships and life-building tools to your children and those living in your world, and through the use of these techniques and positive influence, assertiveness, and effective communication, they will be successful."
~Lee Braddock~

What is positive and negative feedback? How do you use it? How does it affect you? Positive and negative feedback is information that is transferred from one person to another. This information can be about a person, place, thing, or behavior. Positive and negative information/feedback can be either constructive or destructive. If the speaker is an assertive person, the information will always be offered with an educational tone.

The process of giving and receiving positive and negative feedback will create either good or bad behaviors, depending on how it is delivered and perceived. Feedback can be delivered in a manner that belittles, offends, hurts, controls, manipulates, or destroys. It can also be threatening to make the other person feel as though they have been beaten up.

However the best way is to deliver feedback is in an educational manner, to nurture, build self-esteem and confidence, etc. Your intent will dictate how positive or negative feedback is delivered.

You have all experienced hurtful feedback that was belittling or insulting. This type of feedback causes anger and creates physical and emotional abuse. It can create resentment to the point of wanting revenge. Many of you have experienced individuals that argue and fight until someone finally gives in. They simply will not give up or shut up until you concede that *they* are right! These people are referred to as *"Right Fighters."* If you find that you can't reason with them, then avoid them. Generally, you will not be able to reason with a Right Fighter.

These argumentative ways of communicating are physically and emotionally exhausting. Through means of effective communication, the receiving or giving of feedback should never be offered in a negative fashion. However, again, this is your choice! We can beat this person to a pulp verbally, or we can educate them. It would be prudent to examine your intent before communicating feedback.

What are the advantages of beating someone up, in comparison to what you may gain from teaching them and encouraging them? Think for a moment how you would like to receive feedback. Do you want someone to brow beat you, belittle, hurt, or insult you, or would you prefer that someone be kind enough to educate you?

I hope you have learned so far, that being assertive is not simply communication. It is also behaviorally based. It is being kind, loving, thoughtful, and encouraging, not just to others, but to ourselves, as well. All through this book, I have explained how we influence others and do not control them; this is simply a choice of behaviors. It's how we treat others and how we want them to treat us that should be our focus.

Through the process of giving and receiving feedback, we engage in a valuable learning process. If we pay attention to it, whether given in an appropriate way or not, it is our choice and we can learn from it all!

Note: In many circumstances, I have found that feedback is given with the intent of controlling another or is meant to be used as a manipulative tool. Our personal responsibility is to discern their intent and consider the information given to us. The person that has the intent of controlling or manipulating us will use vague data, so we need to examine what they are saying. If necessary ask for clarification and watch their body language. A rule of thumb to go by is if what someone is saying appears different from what their body language (actions) is saying, a red flag should go up quickly because they are not being honest with you (in most situations). If this is the case, pay close attention to their actions because these will reflect the truth and will ultimately protect you. These individuals want to control and manipulate you. Their intent is for you to live according to their judgments, standards, and desires; do not fall into this trap.

ACCEPTING FEEDBACK

Question: What are some of the roadblocks that prevent you from accepting feedback?

If your childhood or adult life has been filled with physical and/or emotional abuse, then accepting positive feedback or compliments can be difficult. It becomes even more arduous to accept when it is negative feedback. You'll most likely possess a strong curiosity about the motive for a compliment, so you instinctively dismiss the accolade. If the feedback is negative, the one who possesses the passive personality type will take the feedback and use it against themselves!! This is typical of someone with a low self-esteem.

It's important to examine the cognitive distortions that have been instilled in us from our past experiences. Again, neurolinguistics estimate approximately 77% of our core beliefs to be negative or distorted. These distortions are the opinions, thoughts, and beliefs of someone else who assisted in the creation of the cognitive distortions we possess about ourselves.

Beware of these distortions and understand them so you are less likely to fall victim or allow them to control your life. Use the tools in this book to examine and change your perceptions to enable you to move forward. Believing and living by the distorted thoughts and beliefs of others allows them to dictate how you should live and feel. The passive person with a low self-esteem continues the emotional abuse that has been inflicted upon them. This behavior causes further destruction to the person's self-esteem and self-worth. They will eventually lose their sense of self as they lose their identity and individualism. These people feel as though they want to disappear...to become invisible. It creates dysfunction in relationships and destroys them.

If we fear being hurt by another, a boyfriend, husband, girlfriend, or wife, we allow them to implant their ideas, thoughts, and behaviors into us. If we are in a one-sided relationship and are holding to a feeling or belief that we can change them or have a responsibility to change them, we are headed for heartbreak! We will do whatever it takes to maintain a stress free relationship, even if it goes against our better judgment or causes us to give up our identity. This type of relationship controls the passive personality. The more negative the feedback you receive, the more you will devalue yourself.

Set reciprocal boundaries and communicate them to everyone, then enforce them. Fear plays an enormous part in the development of our behaviors. Remember, fear is a form of insecurity. Therefore, it is imperative for us to trust and believe in ourselves. It is extremely important to learn the proper tools and techniques to ensure that you learn the best behaviors possible, and in doing so, you create a healthy and happy life.

Do you think it is a sign of conceit to accept a compliment? It is not! An honest compliment comes from the heart of another. It is their belief that created the compliment in the first place, and that belief came from what they personally have witnessed in you. Therefore, it is okay to believe and trust in their compliment.

There are people who feel they will become indebted to the person offering the compliment; this is a myth. If you have low self-esteem, low confidence, or low self-worth, this is the image you possess of yourself. When you are given a compliment it is natural to feel or believe the compliment does not fit your particular self-image and you will automatically reject it. Understand that this is yet another reason to respect the reality of others.

TACTICS USED TO REJECT COMPLIMENTS:

One technique we use is one we learned from childhood, and our children have learned from us; it's called *"selective hearing."* This means that we select or choose those things we want or do not want to listen to, which ultimately leads to the other techniques that are utilized. If we hear something we do not want to hear, we might decide to ignore it and pretend it was never said. There again, we might decide to deny what we've heard and reply that it isn't so.

With the denial technique, we may automatically engage in an argument attempting to convince the giver they are wrong. This argument might continue for some time until the giver concedes. Now, you have become a *"right fighter."*

You might engage into a passive-aggressive questioning process, hoping to create doubt about the judgment of the compliment giver. Another modality is making a joke out of the compliment, which allows you to sidestep and ease your feelings of having to reject the compliment and the compliment giver.

If your self-esteem is in really bad shape, you'll fall into the trap of insulting yourself. You'll attempt to over shadow the compliment with the self-induced insults you inflict upon yourself. This is related to the negative self-talk we discussed earlier. You may possibly go to the other extreme of being passive—aggressive and use self-induced insults to gain more compliments, which can be a double-edged sword.

You might be gracious and accept the compliment, but then you'll employ a tactic of what is referred to as *narrowing*. In other words, you find a way to reduce the compliment to fit your own negative perception of yourself. You may also perform a tactic called *mirroring*. When approached with a compliment, those who mirror feel obligated to return an equal or greater compliment to the giver. This shifts the focus from you to the compliment giver, allowing you to feel justified in accepting the original compliment. Can you see the waste of time and energy that goes along with these types of head games? Wouldn't it be more relaxing and calming to just simply accept the compliment and feel good about it? If we accept the compliment graciously, it would be a positive movement toward a healthy relationship.

When the recipient of the compliment uses these concepts and techniques, it is important to think about and try to understand how they might affect the sincere compliment giver. It is essential to respect the reality of others. It is necessary to understand that you do not have to agree nor do you need to like it; you must, however, respect it. By respecting one's reality, you acknowledge and allow this person the freedom to feel, think, dream, and choose as long as it doesn't interfere with your life and freedoms. Do you not agree?

Using the previous rejection techniques will be an insult to the giver. It suggests that this person has no importance, has poor judgment, has little or no value, and certainly does not know what they are talking about. It also tells the compliment giver that their feelings, opinions, thoughts, ideas, etc., have no validity, and they too are as worthless as you feel about yourself. Compliments are positive feedback. If you reject the feedback that has been given to you, are you not in a sense beating this person up, as you have been beaten up in the past? Ask yourself if this was your intent? Do you want to treat others as badly as you have been treated? I truly hope you do not.

If you are completely sure the compliment given is hype, then you have a right to express your displeasure and confront this person in an assertive manner. Consider this; before you engage in this particular act, ask yourself what harm it would cause if you simply said, thank you, and moved on?

UNDERSTANDING HOW REJECTING COMPLIMENTS AFFECT YOU PERSONALLY

To a certain degree, you already possess low self-esteem, low self-worth, little or no self-respect, little or no self-confidence, and little or no personal value. Rejecting compliments shows little or no trust in your own opinions and thoughts, and places little or no value on those of others. By rejecting compliments, you continue to maintain and perpetuate the self-destructive feelings and thoughts you have about yourself. Would you like to stop? Can you turn these negatives around to a positive by accepting an honest sincere compliment? Yes, you can!

Compliments and feedback in general are gifts to be accepted or rejected by you. Yes, you have a choice, whether you want to accept or reject them. Keep in mind the more you reject feedback, the longer you will remain stagnated in your present life position. If you have read this far, I don't believe you want to continue that behavior.

Limit your associations to those people who love, respect, and care for who and what you are, and not for what others want you to be. This is the beginning of emotional freedom!

Question: What is it that prevents you from giving feedback?

Here again, it has to do with the cognitive distortions, the destructive behaviors and beliefs that we learned throughout our life, as to how and why we feel the way we do about ourselves. If you possess a strong negative perception of yourself, you will always focus on the negative. By doing this, you allow yourself to justify, rationalize, intellectualize, believe, and accept all the negative propaganda you have been indoctrinated with throughout your life. Is it worth the ruined relationships, lost jobs, depression, sadness, self-loathing, and lost dreams just to hang on to those opinions? Each of us has the right to choose a better life for ourselves and our children, and we are the only one that can choose.

All feedback, whether negative or positive can be a healthy

thing. It depends on how it is given and what the speaker's intent is. Most importantly, it is how you wish to perceive the feedback that really counts. Remember to keep in mind the only thing we are empowered to control is ourselves and how people and situations affect us. Regardless whether it is negative or positive feedback, it is advisable to control how it affects us, and to use it as a learning tool. We have the control to allow it to hurt us or not.

A strong, negative perception of ourselves is nothing more than social propaganda. Offering good, healthy, positive feedback offers the recipient a validation of their feelings, emotions, efforts, and skills. If you deal with all feedback in an appropriate way, it will allow you to create positive relationships and a stronger self-esteem. It will also boost your confidence. I mentioned earlier that feedback can be educational, so learn from it. You can learn new behaviors, skills and attitudes, and you can learn new and exciting ways of perceiving life.

This author believes that for anyone to effectively learn, it is extremely important to maintain an open mind and heart, and eliminate prejudices toward other persons and ideas. Respecting one's reality will allow you to increase your ability to see things from a fairer and unobstructed perception. Eventually, this will bring about what you need to facilitate your goals.

GUIDELINES TO ASSIST YOU IN GIVING POSITIVE FEEDBACK

If you follow these tips, it will be easier for you to offer both positive and negative feedback to others without being offensive or hurtful and thereby gaining respect and credibility. It is important that any feedback you offer be honest and accurate. Offer feedback based on one's behavior or one's actions... one's complete act. What I mean by complete act is, if someone does a job they started out doing well, but the majority of the job turned out badly or was incomplete, don't compliment them only on the part that went well. You are not teaching them anything. Be honest in your observations; this creates positive feedback.

Don't offer backhanded feedback, which is loaded with insults. Be specific, be honest and encouraging, but most of all, be real. This is applicable to all relationships. Have you ever heard the old saying, *"if you don't have anything good to say, say nothing at all?"* This is a basic rule of assertiveness. By offering negative feedback in an educational way, you create trust and respect.

Question: What is the value of negative feedback?

Giving and receiving positive feedback is rather easy, and in most cases, it is enjoyable. On the other hand, negative feedback is information that we don't particularly wish to hear. This information may be disappointing or hurtful and sometimes will be unbearable for you to hear. It is also very difficult to deliver.

The purpose of negative feedback is to entice you to take a closer look at those behaviors, attitudes, and actions that causes you negative results. It allows you an opportunity to accept and acknowledge your personal responsibility and accountability while enabling you to take steps toward improving and making positive changes.

Considering that most of us have no idea how to deliver feedback, it is even more imperative we take the responsibility of learning how to control the effect it has on us. Negative feedback can come across as being abusive, causing emotional upheaval. It may also cause one to experience low self-esteem, diminished confidence and social skills, and may create resentments and hurtful memories. These also fuel those old tapes we experience that have a tendency of controlling us. Again, if you control how this feedback affects you, although it may be hurtful, you can sort through it and choose what is truly helpful and educational. One way to do this is to separate yourself from the criticism and focus on what is being said, not from whom it is being said. In other words, **do not take it personally**! Believe me, this is not always easy, but it does work and can be very informative and educational. Facing your bad behaviors and mistakes is not easy to do, but is necessary. You can accomplish this by utilizing your rights, boundaries, and self-talk, and by utilizing your time, place, and rehearsal, and respecting others' reality. When you successfully do this, the feedback has changed from negative to positive. It is an educational tool. Embrace it and use it for your improvement.

None of us really knows how we truly act in everyday situations until we are offered some form of feedback. Most everyone assumes they act appropriately and non-offensively. This concept can be very helpful and fulfilling if you allow it. When we choose to pay attention, negative feedback offers guidance and validation. By paying attention, it offers insight to those areas in our behavior that may need correcting.

CRITICISM

Criticism is commonly viewed as negative feedback and is based on negativity. It is fault finding and a form of disapproval. Criticism is the tool you can use to see yourself as you really are, if properly viewed. It can also be very distorted as well, which may affect your frame of mind. It can create depression, frustration, anger, and other disruptions to your mood. This type of feedback can deliver unrealistic or unfair expectations; these are expectations others project on to you. Sometimes these expectations are self-imposed. They expect you to live, think, and believe in a way they desire for you...for their purpose, not yours.

Criticism is commonly and tragically used to control and manipulate others; it is used primarily by the Passive-Aggressive and Aggressive personalities. The Passive-Aggressive personality is more surreptitious in nature, where the Aggressive personality is bolder than most.

Jealousy is one of those manipulative tools that may be used against us. If we display a Passive or Passive-aggressive personality type, we experience issues with our self-esteem and our confidence level. People will use criticism to attack us, to create guilt, shame, self-doubt, inadequacies, and to make us feel as though we are a failure. Remember, failure does not exist! It is nothing more than a manipulative and controlling tool.

There are three main issues that influence criticism in a negative way. The first is competition. How many times have you been in some form of competition, when a fellow competitor, in either a jovial or vicious way, begins to throw some form of negative criticism your way? If you allow yourself to be sucked into that competitive dialogue, it can have an adverse affect on your performance and thought processes. The purpose for this kind of criticism is meant to break your concentration causing you to give up your own control, which can create anger.

Competition will also cause frustration from time to time. Competition causes us to become frustrated with our existing circumstances, which may result in stuffing those feelings of frustrations until our performance is negatively altered or we blow-up.

The last one is the most severe and has more adverse affects on us... It is fear, the affects of which can be devastating. It causes us to beat around the bush, avoid getting to the point, and to sidestep our decision-making. It will cause us to doubt our abilities and ultimately quit, or give up. This makes most people feel as though they have failed! ***Failure does not exist! It only exists in the mind of the giver!***

"*Watch your thoughts; they become words.*
Watch your words; they become actions.
Watch your actions; they become habits.
Watch your habits; they become character.
Watch your character; it becomes your destiny."

~Frank Outlaw ~

CHAPTER **10**

The Different Forms of Criticism

Non-Verbal Criticism:

There are 4 major forms of criticism; non-verbal, indirect, direct, and hostile. Approximately 95% of all communications is non-verbal. Remember, non-verbal communication is body language and facial expressions, and includes physical movements used in response to what we hear, see, and feel. We might hear, see, or feel something that we disagree with or simply dislike. Therefore, our non-verbal response might be to look away, roll our eyes, fold our arms across our chest, cross our legs, or we might become frustrated and begin tapping our fingers, foot, or just walk away. What does this body language tell you about what you are feeling? Did the information make you nervous or upset?

These non-verbal characteristics are extremely valuable in reading how we affect others with whom we are communicating. If we are attentive to these signs, we will become more astute at identifying these characteristics and more able to make adjustments in our speech and behaviorisms. We are more apt to control our frustration, anger, and confusion simply *by adjusting how we listen* to the information.

Within the realm of non-verbal criticism, body language is a device that many have utilized as a technique to control or manipulate a person's behaviors, thoughts, and beliefs. Non-verbal communication can be a very powerful tool if used for the improvement of ourselves and others.

INDIRECT CRITICISM

Indirect criticism is more often accepted as being politically correct. This author believes that by being politically correct, we avoid accepting responsibility and commitment. One will dance around the real issue and never commit, one way or the other. This is a convenient way for Passive-Aggressive personalities to sidestep responsibility and accountability. When looking at society as a whole, most people are Passive-Aggressive. In this form, it is easy to deliver up backhanded compliments filled with an unspecified intent. It appears positive at first, but retains a negative message. As the receiver, you may be offended or hurt by the remarks and the giver will deny any hurtful substance. It has been my experience that this is commonly used by those in corporate environments, politics, by addicts, supervisors, and those in domestic violence situations. They simply do not want to commit or accept responsibility.

HOSTILE

This form is drenched in aggression. These people assume an aggressive posture and utilize behaviors that will invade your personal space. They might attempt to tower over you to intimidate or control you. Their vocal tones and inflections will be strained and raised, and they may attempt to stare you into submission.

If these methods are not working well for them, they will become verbal, insulting, and belittling to you, and may also attack you verbally to gain control over you. The results of these actions cause cognitive distortions, which are the beginning of self-destructive behaviors we will adopt. They attempt to out-talk you and will rationalize, justify, and intellectualize until they win. This is very similar to the right fighter.

If you think back to earlier relationships when someone aggressive used these techniques on you, did you begin to second guess yourself? Did you begin to question your self-confidence, self-esteem, and your personal value? This is the most dangerous and destructive form of criticism.

DIRECT CRITICISM

Direct criticism is without a doubt the most effective, open, honest, and reliable form of communication we have. This is done without any aggression and creates an environment that allows us to become the assertive person we want to be.

This is an assertive form of communication. As I said earlier, at one time or another everyone will run through every personality type at some point in their lives because it's human nature to do so.

However, we must focus our core behavior on being assertive at all times. At times, when we are in a passive or an aggressive mode, we might become overly emotional. This is okay as long as we are aware of what is going on, and we make the appropriate adjustments.

Being direct goes against the unreasonable expectations of others and is also the easiest type to deal with. It is less stressful, less frustrating, and creates much less anxiety. It is also less offensive. Think of someone in your life that brings forth much negative feedback toward you and think about how you could handle it assertively. Then write this plan of action down for later review.

HOW DO YOU REACT TO CRITICISM?

I don't know of anyone who enjoys listening to negative criticism, no matter how it is offered. Words, smells, tastes, and hearing instills certain feelings, thoughts, memories, and fears into us. When you hear words of criticism or confrontation, it usually evokes feelings of doubt, anxiety, worry, anger, defensiveness, and fear. If we stop for a moment and do our best to understand what these words imply, we will thwart many of the negative feelings that invade our sensibilities and allow us to feel more confident. Then, if we attempt to understand what the feelings are and where they are coming from, we might be able to get a handle on what the truth is. This is one of those times where it might be important to utilize time, place, and rehearsal.

Let's look at how doubt affects us. When being criticized, do you think about your failures? Do you begin doubting yourself and your abilities because of the negative and hurtful propaganda you endured in your life? Will you begin to experience feelings of guilt or shame? Where does that come from... Why?

Simplistically and accurately, guilt denotes that we have _done_ something. It also shows intent. Keep in mind that if you begin to rationalize and justify these feelings of guilt instead of looking at the facts, you'll talk yourself into feeling guilty for the rest of your life. Examine specifically what you have _done_ to feel guilty about? Write these things down so that you can go back later to appraise them objectively.

However, if you have done something that has caused you to feel guilt or shame, face up to it, take responsibility for your actions, and make amends.

Note: As a child, I felt ashamed because I believed I was stupid. I believed I could do nothing right. I was constantly reminded that I was worthless, irresponsible, and incapable of doing anything well. Shame and guilt create horrible feelings of inadequacy, cause low self-esteem, self-doubt and personal value is decreased. It automatically brought my confidence level down, and thwarted my ability to respond effectively (communicate) to the negative criticism being delivered. So I unconsciously believed and accepted whatever was being said, regardless of whether it was accurate or not.

Write these things down so you can go back later to examine

them objectively. In reality, people should only feel guilty when they have actually done something to offend or hurt someone else. An honest mistake is not a reason to feel guilty or shameful, it merely calls for an apology and a correction. We must examine our intent and look at the speaker's intent as well. Ask for clarification. Do not take things at face value, even if you know this person is well intended; examine their intent. Respect the reality of others! You do not have to like or accept it, you should simply respect it.

The same goes for shamefulness. What kind of person are you? Are you stupid, lazy, and worthless? The answer is *"NO."* Examine who you really are and understand what makes you tick. Why should you feel shame and guilt? Is it because someone else wants you to feel shameful or guilty, so they can manipulate or control you?

Note: If you would commit to accepting yourself as a human being who will continue to make mistakes and commit to making a concerted effort to learn from those mistakes, you will greatly minimize those feelings of shame and guilt. Remember, if you respect the reality of others and appropriately listen to the criticism being offered, you *"DO NOT"* have to defend your beliefs to anyone. You owe no one an explanation, unless you choose to give it.

You do not have to hear someone say that you are stupid or worthless to feel or believe that you are. These feelings and opinions are conveyed to us by the way we are treated, i.e. body language. Therefore, who are you that you should allow someone to make you feel shameful, guilty, or inadequate? These are very important issues to think about and consider. Understand that no one can make you feel shameful, guilty, or even inadequate, unless you allow them to do so! Remember, I said earlier that there are people who are very proficient with these tools (assertiveness) and use them to get even with those who have hurt them? I caution you not to do this!

When anger sets in, it is common for one to counterattack the criticizer with negative criticism or insults, which ultimately keeps these issues open and festering with no resolution in sight. We will eventually get into what I refer to as an endless *pissing match*. If we are incapable of dealing with certain issues, we may deny their existence, or they might go into denial.

Addicts live in a state of denial about their addiction. Domestic abusers deny the abuse they impose. This is a trap so easy to fall into that you can fool yourself and others into believing this is a form of assertiveness, when it's nothing more than a denial of reality.

If we are truly correct in our thinking and feeling, why would we have a need to convince anyone we are right and they are wrong? Could it be that you have a deep feeling of insecurity in your heart or that you doubt yourself? If that is the case, it would be important in your mind to convince others you are right.

Getting defensive is another trap we fall into. This denial will force us into becoming a right fighter. This is a person who will argue until they turn blue in the face trying to convince you they are right, even when all the facts appear otherwise. It doesn't matter if this person is right, wrong, or indifferent, he or she will argue until you concede. If you find yourself in this position, ask yourself, do I want to be right or do I want to be happy? We can never be right all the time; however, we can be happy the majority of our lives. Which of these is more acceptable to you?

Anger accompanies anxiety, confusion, and worry. Anger can be a healthy emotion if used appropriately. The problem arises when it is used inappropriately and we get stuck in that emotion.

When you have a bad day, do you take your frustrations out on others that do not deserve it? As with most people, I know I have. Have you had moments where something insignificant concerning something someone said or did, sets you off? When we allow our anger to fly, we allow the anger to control our thought processes and our actions and relationships are damaged. This prevents us from doing anything positive. When anger takes control of us, we have to work 10 times harder to move ahead because we have to repair the damage we've done, and then make up for lost time.

We have talked about setting reciprocal boundaries for our personal protection as well as that of our families. Anger does quite the opposite. It builds walls and barriers around us that need to be brought down in order to move forward. Anger is the father of resentment! Anger has a tremendous effect on how we think and feel, and how we treat others and ourselves, sometimes for very long-periods of time.

Our thought processes are made up of imagination and creativity. Our ability to reason and think logically, to problem solve and make decisions are either tempered or ignited by these characteristics. This is what assists us in becoming successful in life, or it can destroy us. These will be stopped or at least impaired by anger. Impairing our thought processes will prevent us from succeeding and diminish our ability to be compassionate, understanding, and loving. Our ability to find balance in life is hampered, as well. Anger is the catalyst that destroys progress. Inappropriate anger is the assassin of our souls.

Fear is a powerful motivator. What is it that we are fearful of? Is it rejection, success, confrontation, or maybe finding out that you are not the person you hoped you were? If we accept ourselves, how can we be rejected or feel rejection?

Confrontation will be discussed more in detail later in this book, but many people are extremely fearful of this. Success is nothing more than how one person defines it for themselves; it can be one's perception, or it can also be determined by reaching or not achieving certain goals. To one person, success may be defined as having millions of dollars. To another it may be having power over life and death, or by how many lives one has touched in a positive way.

Success to me means that I have ensured that my wife and family are happy and healthy, and that I am a good husband, father, and friend. This may not seem very ambitious to some, but if you clearly understand what this goal means to me, it is a tall order that most people over look or are incapable of achieving because of the commitment involved. If in my classes and individual sessions, my writings and lectures are able to help someone, then I am a success. I believe it is important to examine what kind of legacy we will leave, because it will have a direct influence on everyone we touch. If I know I have provided someone the opportunity to improve their lives and/or relationships, then I am a success! All those things I have no control over I leave in God's hands. This allows me to have a more stress free life and more enjoyable relationships.

Criticism is nothing more than an exchange of information; a form of communication... feedback, if you will. It is sharing one's perceptions. You do not have to agree with it, like it, or accept the information; however, you must respect that person's right to communicate their opinion. This is the reality we discussed that needs to be respected. Considering the brief explanations on this subject, does this give you more or less confidence in dealing with criticism? It is my desire that it will.

"I've learned that no matter what happens, or how bad it seems today, life does go on, and it will be better tomorrow."

~Maya Angelou~

CHAPTER **11**

Tools and Techniques to Minimize Fear and Anger

Several tools and techniques can be used to minimize fear and anger. I suggest you try them all and pick those that will work for you in most situations. Many of these strategies are derived from our minds; therefore, it is imperative we be aware and listen to our bodies.

Learn to relax, using deep breathing or mind relaxation techniques. As discussed earlier, stress and anxiety cause frustration and anger. These cause your body to react negatively. It alters your posture, vocal speed, tones, inflection, and your breathing. If the anger is elevated, you may even clench your fists and jaw. Then your muscular system tightens and prevents you from thinking clearly. If you use a breathing technique to relax, this will help stifle the affects of the anger to a certain degree, or at least to a level where you can begin thinking clearly again.

Avoid retaliation! This is sometimes very difficult to accomplish. However, it can be done with much practice and a lot of patience. When we feel anger coming upon us, focus on what the real issue is that is causing the anger. Do not allow yourself to be sidetracked by anger, negative talk, or the introduction of other issues! Usually these other issues have little or nothing to do with what is being discussed.

People have a tendency to push buttons in others that cause

anger. Therefore, if you maintain your vigilance and remain focused, you will find that many times the real issues are filled with nonsense.

Note: The biggest reason others may push your buttons is to cause you to become angry, which allows them to control you more easily. This is one of the greatest controlling tools there are. If you think about what we discussed concerning anger, you can see the logic in this statement. If you can anger someone, you can also escalate or deescalate their anger. We used to practice this principle as children with our siblings; we called it teasing. I used to tease my younger brothers and sister quite a bit, although teasing is a milder form of pushing buttons.

This next strategy is equally important. Recall your personal needs; one of which is your safety. It is essential to be very much aware of your surroundings, avoid any hints of violent behavior or attitudes. We can do this by communicating as assertively as possible and using all the techniques available. For instance, we can utilize time, place and rehearsal and refrain from making "you" statements and asking "why" questions.

Accept yourself as being a fallible human being, which means you will make mistakes. Therefore, you should not demand perfection from others or yourself. If you accept that the majority of the world does not know how to deliver negative feedback or effectively communicate with others, then you need to accept the responsibility of picking out the important information that is needed. This will be discussed further when we talk about open-ended questions.

We've talked about respecting the reality of others. An effective way of doing this is to validate or restate the critic's perception. Again, by respecting one's perception or reality, does not mean you are required to like it, accept it, or agree with it. It only means that you allow this other person the right to have their own opinions, thoughts, and beliefs. This is their right, just as it is yours. Validate their feelings and emotions. By respecting one's reality and validating their feelings and emotions, you will defuse, or at least minimize, any anger and frustration that might exist, which will enable you to get the real issues out in the open for discussion. As you are *"actively listening,"* don't be afraid to agree with those issues that you really do agree with. Agreeing doesn't mean the critic will think you are changing your opinion, or that you are caving in, it only means there are some issues in which you both agree. Likewise, this is telling the other person that they are not completely wrong and you don't fully disagree. I use this concept of, *"agreeing in part,"* as a therapist, as it allows me to pick out information that lets me go through the backdoor, so-to-speak. It enables me to prevent their anger from rising because it validates the individual.

People who are good communicators use the concept of *"wait and listen."* Therapists use this all the time; it is very effective and educational. If you wait and listen when asking open-ended questions, you allow the speaker to think about their behaviors and opinions. This is what you want to happen. By allowing the speaker to complete his/her thoughts and statements, you are paying them respect. By paying them respect, it is very likely they will reciprocate. When you actively listen, you learn volumes about this person and how to achieve what you need.

While waiting and listening, you may realize most people are, at best, ambiguous. I refer to this ambiguity in part as being politically correct. These people hardly ever get to the point and appear to dance around the issue as they avoid making a solid commitment. This is another way of avoiding responsibility. Therefore, it makes sense that these types of people criticize you on how they perceive an event, not on the event itself. So it might behoove you to get clarification and specify exactly what the criticism is about. If you are given indirect or non-verbal criticism, utilize your personal rights and request clarification. If they refuse to clarify, this is their right, as well.

Keep in mind the three things we are empowered to control.

Do you remember what they are? You can only control *yourself*, and how *people* and *situations* affect you.

In a situation where someone has requested clarification or explanation from you, it is okay to comply. However, you do not have to offer excuses or defend your reasoning. This is one of your personal rights. Believe in yourself and your explanation. Be confident of who you are and what you feel. Be willing to change your opinions or beliefs if you are shown that you are wrong. It is okay to be mistaken!

One problem I believe people fall victim to from time to time, is working to *convince or change the minds of others* to your point of view or beliefs. There could be a number of things going on. It could be a feeling of personal doubt, insecurity or even worse; it could be considered a form of control and or manipulation. Avoid this type of behavior as it can cause damage to a relationship. It does not mean you are a bad person. It may appear this person is a *"right fighter,"* but it could simply be that you have so much passion for something that it blinds your good sense and intent.

For some reason, people *(most often women)* feel that they can change someone they care about or love. **This is not true... It is a myth!** People will only change if *they* choose to, not before. Don't put yourself in a position where others will get angry or where you cause yourself grief because you are attempting to change someone else and meeting up with an immovable wall... It's not worth it! This behavior causes huge problems and resentments.

As an assertive person, you will find thanking your critic is very much appropriate, because it commands respect for you. The difference between demanding respect versus commanding respect is simple. One who demands respect does not feel as though they need to earn it. These are aggressive people and they expect others to show them respect, regardless of their actions. Those who command respect earn it through their actions and positive influence, nothing more. These are assertive people. Thanking someone for their feedback does not necessarily mean you have to agree with the critique, or that you have to like it. It only means that you respect them for offering their opinion. This type of behavior is very powerful.

If you run up against someone who has the intention of hurting or insulting you, remember that you can only control how people affect you. Therefore, you may respond by utilizing your right to speak your displeasures, and with a respectful attitude and behavior, advise them that you do not appreciate their comments. You do not have to listen to it or associate with this type of person. Then leave and avoid any attempt of being sucked into an argument.

In a situation where there appears to be some confusion, use your right to request time to think before responding. During this time-period, it is highly advisable for you to rehearse what you want to say and how you want to say it. This will increase your confidence level and self-esteem, and you are assured to get the information out and delivered the way you intend. These strategies or techniques are your tools to use to protect yourself. Get proficient with them and use them daily! You will be pleasantly surprised at the results.

"People may doubt what you say or even doubt
what you are, but they always believe in what you do."

~Author Unknown~

CHAPTER 12

What Situations Require Communicating Constructive Feedback

We have looked at positive and negative feedback and how each can be delivered. It has been explained that even positive feedback can be delivered in a negative fashion to where one may feel as though they have been beaten up. It can also be delivered in such a way that one might be educated and built up emotionally.

Because it is difficult and somewhat fearful to listen to feedback, especially negative, it is important you learn to give and receive all forms of feedback in a productive manner. Without constructive feedback, all relationships deteriorate.

Every form of feedback can have enormous influence on you. It is important to think about the outcome it has on others and on you individually. We will receive and deliver feedback in the workplace, at home, in school, within all our relationships, or in our day to day communications with the general public. Every time feedback is given or received, it needs to be positive, educational, and supportive, regardless of the situation or circumstances that exist.

Feedback delivered in this manner will improve all relationships. Additionally, school will be more acceptable to kids, relationships will be strengthened, and work will be less stressful. Respect is developed and nurtured in all of these areas.

Note: It has been determined that the last thing said, is usually what is remembered! So, deliver information, *NOT ADVICE*. When you deliver information, you give others a choice. You empower them with information; however, offering advice may disempower them. Lastly, you should not allow your emotions to guide or control you, and you should not personalize things. These make us more cognizant of the feelings of others and will help us to respect their reality. This is assertiveness! Therefore, it is important to use constructive or positive feedback every time, regardless of the magnitude or reason.

HOW DISCOMFORT WORKS AGAINST US.

There are two common pitfalls people use that cause various levels of discomfort. Be aware of these so you can avoid falling into them. *"Ambiguity"* is the vagueness, the uncertainty, or the doubt we feel. This causes confusion, and to other people we will appear to be wishy-washy.

At times, ambiguity may cause fear and anger. We may be in a situation where we have to make a decision. We feel doubt and uncertainty, then we feel pressured into making a decision we're not ready to make. We become fearful or angry as our emotions turn toward feeling that we are being forced into making a decision. The feelings of fear or anger are those of control and manipulation.

Ambiguity many times forces us into avoidance. *"Avoidance"* is the act of evasion, evading, escaping, or dodging. These actions are most common when it comes to one's feelings, emotions, and responsibilities. Avoidance is usually the first action caused by your fear and anger. At all costs, you must not avoid problems or responsibilities because it can lead to disaster. Avoidance causes you to become politically correct and leads you to avoid making any type of commitment. If you examine the reasons for *"avoidance,"* it boils down to your personal fear of making the wrong decision. Many times you decide simply by not deciding… Does this make

sense? When you are so fearful or confused about making a decision and you decide to wait, you have really made a decision to
remain status quo; do you agree? This lack of decision-making
may well be a bad choice, because if you are in a physically and
emotionally abusive relationship, not making a decision can be
dangerous for yourself or others in the household.

Ambiguity and avoidance will provoke aggression. When we
feel confused, frustrated, or pushed into a corner or we feel we
are being avoided, we may feel aggression coming on. If we feel
uncomfortable about giving or receiving feedback, it is common
to get angry. It is important to become comfortable with the giving
and receiving of all forms of feedback using a good attitude so
that your message is perceived.

"I've learned that people will forget what you said, people will forget what you did, but people will never forget how you made them feel."

~Maya Angelou~

CHAPTER 13

The Most Powerful Word in Existence

What is the most powerful word in your life? *"NO!"* This is a word many, many people do not understand and are simply afraid to use. If people truly understood the power of this word, it would be used more often, because most generally it is used incorrectly and selfishly.

Have you ever asked yourself what this word truly means? Have you ever considered how much power this word possesses? A simple two letter, one syllable word has so much power it can actually alter your life and your relationships. Most of society have difficulty telling others, *no*. In my own family this word is not only difficult to say, but to enforce. It is equally challenging for many people to live up to. Passive, passive-aggressive, and aggressive personality types experience the most difficulty.

Remember, you teach people how to treat you. When you begin to examine the meaning of the word, *"no,"* it is imperative to think about how this word applies to you personally. What influence will this word have on the people in our lives, especially those that take advantage of us and abuse us because of our inability to say no? If we have children, what affect will this have on them and their future? I believe parents use the word, *no*, as an excuse or justification that really does more harm than good.

Note: A word of caution; by the time a child reaches the age of 18, it is estimated they have been told NO approximately one million times. Further, because of its improper use, it has had a negative effect on most children. It is very important to be selective when using this word with our children. If we use the tools in this book and make sure that "no" is used to educate and up build, our negative use will be reduced. It was my responsibility to teach my children how to make decisions and take responsibility for their actions. Therefore, it was a household rule that if their decisions were not going to violate the law or our boundaries at home, and would not cause them or someone else physical injury, they could make their own decisions. It was an increased responsibility on the part of my wife and I, but it paid off in the end.

"No," means to restrict, refuse, rebuff, or offer a negative response, to reject, or to deny, etc. More importantly, if we don't learn to say, no, and defend it, we will not be able to regain control of our lives. For instance, telling someone we are going to reject their abuse is one of our rights as human beings. If we enforce this, will it not protect us? By saying no and enforcing it, are we not setting and enforcing a reciprocal boundary? Will this not help you take control of your life and reshape your future? It is the desire of this author to teach you how to do this.

What prevents you from saying, no? Is it because you privately hope people will **not** ask for anything? Do you fear people will not accept or respect you? Do you believe you don't have a right to say, no? Are you fearful that you are not strong enough to succeed when defending our decision to say "no?" Guilt and shame may also prohibit you from using this word, as well...does any of this sound familiar? Are there other justifications why you don't say, no?

Remember, these tools interact and support one another and need each other to work properly. Being assertive is not just having a positive posture, being confident, or using your choice of time. It is also taking control of our life and saying, no, when necessary. Whatever you do, remember you do not have to apologize for saying no. It will be prudent at times to explain why, but an apology is not necessary. It is okay for others not to accept us because not everyone will. However, it is extremely important that we accept ourselves, for if we do, then others will follow.

Do not attempt to convince anyone of your thoughts, points of view, ideas, or position... just state them. If you believe in yourself, you won't feel a need to convince anyone. Be willing to accept the consequences that might occur from saying no or by standing up for yourself. Let's say you are living with a significant boyfriend or girlfriend. One day they begin to verbally abuse and take advantage of you. You get tired of this behavior and tell them, *"No more!"* Then your significant friend tells you they are going to leave you high and dry. You have to ask yourself if you can live with this consequence. It is advisable to ask yourself this question every time you feel a need to say no. If your answer is, *"yes, I can,"* then move forward and invite them to *hurry up and leave.* People will attempt to control you by making comments that make you fearful. If you are not willing to live with the consequences and you don't set and enforce your boundaries, you will continue to live with abuse.

Let's look at another situation that involves an interfering parent that is causing you great discomfort in your life. You set your boundary and communicate the boundary to them, asking that they stop the behavior. Obviously, there needs to be a consequence for violating that boundary, which you relate to them will be a period in which you will have no contact with them.

After violating your boundary, you step up to enforce the consequence. Appalled at your enforcement, they reply that they will not have anything more to do with you if you follow through with your consequence. What do you do? Do you maintain your *emotional integrity* and enforce your boundary, or do you allow fear to continue to control your life and cause you misery? You know they love you, and in most cases they will cave in sooner or later. By maintaining your integrity, you are teaching them how to treat you, and you are commanding respect from them for being strong enough to defend your rights.

In the event all hell breaks loose and they decide they cannot live with those consequences and want nothing further to do with you... Can you live with that? It may hurt and can be emotionally draining, but, yes, you can! Ask yourself what it is you need to learn from this? If they truly respected you and loved you in the first place, wouldn't they respect your reality, whether they liked it or agreed with it? If you enforce your boundaries, and they rebel, remember that you have a very long time to live with yourself; do you want to be happy or miserable? You and you alone have the primary responsibility to make yourself happy, because no one else will.

You have the right to say no to others, and they have a right to reject it. It is how both parties deal with this and co-operate with one another for a peaceful solution that makes all the difference. I cannot stress enough how you must *"believe"* in yourself. When you say no to someone, you assert your right to make your own decisions, and by doing so, you will achieve a greater amount of satisfaction.

A dilemma many of us have is making a request sound like a request and not an attempt to control anyone. Again, believe in yourself and become comfortable with this. Although it may not be easy to believe, but considering the needs of others will automatically fulfill our own needs.

Make sure you are clear and understand exactly what is needed from this situation or person. Don't be afraid to ask for what you need... It is your right! You do not have to apologize for anything, unless it is necessary, and you'll know whether it is or not. Whatever you do, do not ever put yourself down for requesting what you need. What is not essential is for you to be controlled by another person.

This is why rehearsal is so vitally important. Be careful of the words you use so you don't come across as demanding or controlling. You must trust in yourself before others can learn to trust you. As with belief, forgiveness and love have to start inside you, while accepting the fact that it is **OKAY** to make a mistake. If you are not making mistakes, you are not learning, and you are not moving forward.

Much of this is repetitive information, but as I have said, all of these tools are related and need one another to be effective. I am giving you different analogies to see how they work; one or more will be more meaningful to you than the others. Repetition helps us learn and will subject things to memory.

Take time to write down a description of what you need. Be as clear and precise as possible. Then vocalize your feelings, emotions, and your particular needs aloud. Do not act on them, yet. While still writing them down, focus on those positive feelings, emotions, and needs. Remain calm and confident. Do not rationalize or justify them away or into existence. It is imperative that you are willing to make a commitment to accept responsibility for your own actions, feelings, needs, and behaviors. Do not over-emphasize the bad, and stay clear of the *"me, me, me"* complex; it is a sure relationship killer and is extremely destructive to you and your goals.

It is time to be specific. Specify exactly what you *need* before you act and be willing to accept the consequences. Remember to keep it short, simple, and to the point. People may say, *no,* or they may surprise you and do something you had not anticipated or wanted. You need to continue to be aware of their feelings, concerns, and needs. Being cognizant of the feelings and needs of others does not mean you have to ignore your own needs or put yourself last.

Each of the tools we have gone over thus far are of equal importance. In combination with one another, they are powerful. It may seem there is a lot of information and you might feel somewhat overwhelmed, but I urge you to try and get a handle on them by taking each of them, one at a time, and building on them. Every journey begins with the first step! Good luck.

Maybe God wants us to meet a few wrong people before meeting the right one, so that when we finally meet the person, we will know how to be grateful."

~·Author Unknown~

CHAPTER **14**

The World's Worst and Most Feared Concept

"Confrontation"

As I have said before, understanding is a major key to our existence. When we develop a clear understanding of a word, term, issue, subject, or behavior, it does several things for us. Most importantly it will increase your self-confidence, self-esteem, personal value, and inner strength. It also allows you to find reasonable solutions to your own problems. Instead of being fearful of the term *confrontation*, you should try to develop a clear understanding of it and **embrace** it so your concerns and fears can be reduced.

"Confrontation" is another one of those terms that instills feelings of doubt, fear, negativity, inadequacy, hesitation, avoidance, and much difficulty. I must admit that society has placed a nasty association with it. The majority of people I talk with about this term offer their definition as being aggressive, pushy, negative, and even violent, which is far from the truth. This term does bring out these types of feelings because people do not understand it, nor do they know how to deal with it.

What is confrontation? It is nothing more than *the act of two people coming face-to-face to communicate. It is simply an exchange of information between two or more people.* It doesn't imply anything that resembles aggressiveness, violence, anger, or any other negative. Considering this new explanation, how can this be aggression, violence, or fear? Do you think the feelings this word ignites in most of us are nothing more than cognitive distortions that have been implanted in our minds? The reality is, no one can escape confrontation. If you embrace it, those feelings would change for the better, making the act of confrontation easier to deal with and manage. Usually confrontation involves negative feedback and this is what creates the negatives associated with this word.

Your feelings will dictate your emotions and how you react. So, if you get a negative feeling from a particular term, how are you going to allow it to affect you? Are you going to feel nervous, anticipate trouble, or an argument? Are you going to feel stressed, fearful, or anxious? Are you going to feel threatened or angered, or will you possibly isolate? Many people experience these feelings. What you believe in is what you will create.

If you anticipate trouble, then trouble is not too far behind. We emanate anticipated feelings, and people pick up on them. It is your body language that is being emanated. When someone is fearful of animals, and they approach a dog, the dog instinctively picks up on that fear and reacts to it; people are no different.

This fear or anticipation may stifle your assertiveness and will show up in your body language, giving and receiving feedback, and offering your opinions. It shuts down your ability to say no or to even make requests. This will affect your every relationship with friends, children, and co-workers. Anytime you need to confront someone, these issues will pop up and cause you problems. Consequently, it would behoove you to embrace this term and become comfortable with it. When you were growing up, you were indoctrinated with a misunderstanding of this word. Therefore, do you think a proper understanding will help you change your distorted views?

Areas that can cause confrontation are infidelity, other relationship issues, finances, child rearing, inability to accept personal responsibility, etc. A few of the lesser important issues that might cause confrontation can be the squeezing of the toothpaste tube in the middle or leaving the toilet seat up. The lack of setting reciprocal boundaries and the enforcement of those boundaries perpetuate the negative aspects of confrontation. Fear of confrontation prevents most people from setting and enforcing their boundaries. However, according to its definition, confrontation can be as simple as meeting a friend for lunch and having a friendly conversation.

All the tools discussed throughout this book will reduce your difficulties. As a review, develop a proper use of your time, use the Bonsai Principle; keep it short, simple, and to the point. Learn to actively and empathically listen; be honest and open, and clarify, clarify, clarify. Develop and maintain effective decision-making skills, trust in yourself, increase your self-confidence, and journal daily.

It is important to determine the real issue before communicating it to anyone... Focus on the issue, subject, or behavior... *Not on the person.* Learn to define and determine what your needs are. Always examine your behaviors and if needed, be willing to change them for the better. As I have stated before, we are incapable of solving any problem we cannot or will not identify, acknowledge, and make a commitment to change.

If you are always prepared to confront *(not in an aggressive sense)* strictly for exchanging information, and remember that you have the right to pick your place to confront, your anxiety will be reduced. Practice describing, communicating, and being specific about your needs and examine the outcome. After examining the possible consequences, be willing to accept them. I cannot stress enough that you be very much aware of your personal safety. There will be people who insist on arguing; you do not have to engage them!

Note: We cannot solve perceptions, we can only solve problems. This is your life, take control of it and care about it!

"*Make yourself a better person and know who you are before you try to know someone else and expect them to know you.*"

~Author Unknown~

CHAPTER 15

Living in the Past

"The best predictor of your 'future' is your past!"
~Phillip C. McGraw, Ph.D.~

If you'd like an idea of what your future will look like, take a look at your past and the behaviors that created your past. If you do not like your past, and you want a better future, then you need to change your future past!

Your past is inevitable; you can't escape it. Whether it was a happy, wonderful, and loving past, or if it was filled with hurtful, tumultuous experiences that left physical and emotional scars to carry the rest of your life... It has happened!. If you decide not to change your future, your past will repeat itself, and you will continue to relive the hurt and pain again, and again, and again. However, as an adult you have the choice to instill life-long, healthy changes! In this book are the tools you need; take them and use them.

It is important to change your perception of the past. If you can avoid thinking of your past as painful, hurtful, violent, or abusive, and begin thinking and perceiving the past as a learning tool, you can then use past experiences as an outline for your personal boundaries. Utilize the concepts and tools in this book to instill the changes you desire to achieve that happy and healthy life.

Living in the past is the most dangerous and self-destructive place to be. Before you can move forward with your life, it is very important for you to resolve some of your past issues. This is commonly referred to as one's "baggage." The following diagram shows how behavior is created and will help you understand much about the construction of your past behaviors.

As you think about a particular past issue, begin to analyze it and write down the specific parts in the appropriate column. Take a piece of paper and make three columns, as shown below:

What was the first thought you had that created the negative belief about yourself? Write it down! Example of how this works:

THOUGHTS	FEELINGS	EMOTIONS
{Beliefs}		{Actions & Consequences}
"I'm Stupid"	"Anger"	"Fights" & "School Suspension"

Once you have that written down, examine what feelings came from that belief. Then scrutinize the actions that developed from those feelings. What are the consequences you have experienced? This will help you understand why you feel, act, and think the way you do and can help you find a solution. This is a simple way to see and understand what goes on with your behavior. Look… If you can understand and accept what took place that started those negative thoughts about yourself, you will be able to figure out what changes need to be made to correct them. Generally, these changes are in your personal perception of what and how your past has affected you.

There's a common thread among my clients, regardless of their reasoning for coming to see me… It is their past! Something in that individual's past continues to haunt them and causes dysfunction in their lives, relationships, and employment, etc. No family and no one person is immune from the turbulence of a hurtful past. In my family as a child, I experienced a hurt filled and resentful past. Much of the hurt came from how I perceived it. When I decided to perceive those issues as a learning tool and as something I had no control over, it was easier to accept personal responsibility for my own decisions and actions. I began to implement forgiveness for myself and was able to heal much faster. The changes came from my choices and my commitment to make those changes. I didn't like my past, I certainly didn't like the life I was leading, and I didn't want to relive the experiences of my past.

I have a sibling that continues to suffer from the haunting of his past. His perceptions continue to worsen as the days, months, and years go by. Because he has refused to make the decision to change his perceptions and accept responsibility for his actions, he continues to suffer incessantly. It has destroyed his life, his relationships, and his future. It has destroyed the way he views himself and the way he feels about himself and others; he finds no happiness in anything he does. He places blame on everything and everyone else for his misery. He has difficulty accepting responsibility and accountability for his own actions and hurtful words. His past misery has created a focus in him that disallows anything positive to enter his life or his heart. He created a "me, me, me," complex, where everything is about him and no one else.

Living in the past is a lifelong prison sentence, not only for the victim, but for family members and friends alike. The hurtful memories continue to haunt him, which increases his self-destructive behaviors and feelings. His use of alcohol and marijuana are a major part of the destructive behaviors he demonstrates and he refuses to acknowledge that the use of these materials magnifies his problems. One important thing to understand is the longer time goes by without resolution, the more distorted our perceptions will be of that painful memory.

Every subject discussed in this book is designed to help guide you to actively understand your past issues and find a resolution. The most common statements I hear from family, friends, and colleagues are, "just get over it," "the past is the past," "there is nothing you can do about the past, so forget about it" or, "stop feeling sorry for yourself." These types of statements are very insulting, degrading, and insensitive. The people who utter these remarks have no understanding why people live in their past. As in many cases, these individuals may believe it to be too burdensome and they simply run off at the mouth. It is easier to dismiss one's pain and anguish by using snide remarks.

It could be they have experienced some hurtful events in their own lives that caused them grief and this is their way of subduing the effects of those resentments. You can bet many of these past resentments continue to haunt them because they too have no clear understanding about how to deal effectively with them. This might only barely ease their pain, possibly only temporarily.

As I have said before, we are not typically taught how to problem solve, or how to logically reason, or think through our problems. We are taught how to figuratively sweep problems under the carpet and not talk about them. In either case, they continue to be destructive as long as they are never resolved.

Emotional abuse is the most severe form of abuse. If you never had any intervention, you pick up where the abuser left off as you get older, and even after you leave home. You continue to abuse yourself through those old tapes that keep resonating in your head with negative self-talk, which results in self-destructive behaviors. This is supported and substantiated through the negative criticism victims receive from their family, friends, and society.

With physical abuse, one will heal fairly quickly. On the other hand, emotional abuse has scarred our feelings, lives, and memories, which create hurt, resentment and anger, and fear these will persist as the days, weeks, months, and years go by. The distorted beliefs that one has continue to expand. Many times the original perception of your past is distorted and becomes confused and sometimes forgotten, but the hurt and resentments remain and continue to cultivate. Keep in mind, the longer you go before getting help, the more difficult it is to change, because this negative lifestyle is safer and more comfortable. In fact, any kind of change is filled with uncertainty and fear, and requires a firm commitment to change it.

We rationalize and justify all of our current and past feelings of anger, frustration, hopelessness, confusion and disappointments. As we grow older, feelings of hopelessness and despair increase, which ignites anger and resentments to a higher level. Most of my clients, as well as many others in society turn to the use of alcohol, drugs, food, sex, or other destructive behaviors to counter the hurtful feelings and memories in their lives. Many do not feel worthy of having a happy, healthy relationship, or a satisfying and successful career; they do not believe they deserve anything positive. Their lives are filled with so much anger and resentment, there is no room for anything else.

Our negative past is referred to as *"baggage,"* which is filled with pain, anger, and resentments, and we take them everywhere we go. No matter where you run or hide, you can never escape those hurtful memories and resentments from your past. You become prisoners in your own resentments with a feeling that there is no way out. I have had clients and siblings alike that tell me they are too old to learn something different. They feel they don't have any choices left in life, and they begin to drown in their own misery. They see no light or purpose at the end of their tunnel.

In their state of mind, people perceive them as being filled with self-pity or lazy, or they are viewed as being selfish, manipulative or controlling. The truth is, they are all of these things. The problem is exacerbated by the fact that others do not understand why they are this way, and unfortunately in most cases, they do not care. Remember, it is always easier to ridicule others for their bad behaviors, rather than look at your own issues and commit to fixing them. I find it odd that people will hide, run, fight, and even kill for that which they do not understand.

Many of these people are stuck in their past. They have

become well seated in that lifestyle and oddly enough, feel safe and comfortable there, so they refuse to get help or commit to any effort to change.

I have never met anyone who enjoyed being hateful or hurtful toward anyone. At no time have I known anyone that did not want to be happy. However, I have met many, many people who have given up hope, given up on their dreams, desires, ambitions, families, friends, and jobs because of their past. I expect there are people who disagree with me, and I accept that, but I believe everyone has an obligation to understand their fellow man! I personally believe that everyone has a responsibility to supply the needs of others, because *"understanding"* is the key to our existence.

As a boy growing up, I experienced fist-fights, black eyes, bloody noses, and a even a broken nose a time or two. These healed very quickly and were forgotten as rapidly as they came. However, the emotional and physical abuse I experienced at home took years to understand, and just as long to change. It was due to a lack of understanding on my part and lack of personal commitment to do the work needed for the change to take place. All the way through this book I have said that the most difficult thing to do is to change a lifelong behavior, attitude, or belief.

The best predictor of your future is your past, unless you deliberately and actively choose to change your future past!

HOW DO YOU RESOLVE YOUR PAST EXPERIENCES?

Living in the past is a lifestyle made up of everything that makes you the person you are; your thoughts, dreams, beliefs, ideas, behaviors, attitudes, likes, dislikes, resentments, fears, and all your experiences, whether positive or negative. All these things are what makes you who you are, and more. Each of us has the ability and power to make the changes needed to achieve a happy and healthy existence. If you apply the information in this book, you will have much of the information needed to make positive changes. You can change those areas in your life that need changing to improve the quality of your life; this is a systematic procedure.

I hope you have been taking notes from each section. If not, please go back and review each section, making notes regarding each area of your life that needs to be addressed. The first note to jot down is your personal commitment to yourself to start making positive changes.

Your commitment to change needs to be made in bold letters and said aloud with passion. You might want to say, *"there is nothing that is going to stop me from changing my life, or there is nothing anyone can do or say to stop me from succeeding."* Write it down and put it where you can see it and review it every day. Changing your life is not like anything you have ever done before; it begins first with a commitment, a plan, and then you need to put it into action.

It is extremely important you approach every person and every situation in an individual manner. Do not project your past experiences on to people or situations. Use those negative experiences as a guide and a warning to remind you where you do not want to be, and it will help you succeed.

While dealing with others, if you detect something that gives you the heebie-jeebies, it should throw up a red flag and create caution in you. This is the warning I refer to, nothing more. At this point, take the time to examine the existing circumstances for a conclusion. Do not automatically pre-judge the person or situation in a negative way, else it will always turn out badly. Negativity begets negativity. A red flag allows you the opportunity to choose between either walking away, or taking some positive action, allowing you to utilize time, place, and rehearsal. It will allow you to control your frustrations and anger by placing and enforcing your boundaries. Let these tools assist you in the achievement of an assertive lifestyle.

It is necessary for you to examine several things; first, your self-talk. Reframe the negative self-talk to be more positive. Stay clear of those terms that put doubt in your mind and heart, i.e. *"I think I can, I'll try …, But what if…, I can't do this, This is too hard, I'm not strong enough, I'm not good enough…"* Instead, tell yourself, *"I am going to change my life and become happy and healthy regardless of how difficult it is, or what I need to do to get there… and I refuse to allow anyone to stop me."* In this statement, there is no doubt and no hesitation. There is only a positive affirmation to your personal commitment. Self-talk needs to be done regularly, it is not a one-time thing. Write down the self-talk that is most effective for you in your journal, and review it routinely. There will be times you may need to update your talk… That's okay; it's good to stay flexible!

Much of the negative self-talk used was implanted by others that bullied you and then maintained by you as an adult. For example, if you were picked on in school and other kids instilled in you that you are worthless and no good, or told you things that hurt you and made you feel bad about yourself, these comments have stayed with you throughout your life. When the bullies went their way, and you went yours, you never had resolution, and you likely have picked up where they left off. The hurtful comments will resonate in your thoughts repeatedly for years to come, and they will have a negative impact on your behaviors. It is advisable that you compare these insulting comments to logic. For instance, if someone had convinced you that you are worthless, you need to analyze that statement with logic. Are you worthless? The answer, of course is, "no"! Therefore, you should disregard that comment and change your internal dialogue. It has been my experience that the people who hurt you, whether verbally or physically, are those who live in their own miserable existence and feel a need to make others as unhappy as they feel. *The hurt inflicted on you has nothing to do with you; they are simply attempting to alleviate some of their misery.* Is that fair….absolutely not, but it happens.

It is important for you to prioritize and write down your short and long-term goals. The only difference between a dream and a goal is the **"timeline."** Therefore, write down a date when you would like to achieve your goal. Don't be afraid to be specific, yet realistic, because things happen that will require you to adjust that date, and that's okay. Goals also need to be measurable, so you can see your rate of success.

An example of a short-term goal would be something like this: *"I will set some immediate boundaries that will protect me from my boyfriend's verbal abuse." "I will have this situated properly by the end of the week; or I will have my boundaries set in place to either instill change in them or get rid of them." " I will not hesitate to enforce these boundaries, at any cost, because I have a right to be happy and safe."*

An example of a long-term goal would be, *"I will have increased self-esteem to a recognizable level within 90 days,"* or *"I will create an open, honest, effective communication line with my children by the end of this year."*

Review your rights during this process and give them much consideration, then write down those that will protect and nurture you. If you come up with more personal rights not in this book, write those down as well. The rights that are most important to you are going to dictate what your boundaries will be, how you will communicate those boundaries, and to whom you will communicate them. It will also include how you are going to enforce those boundaries and what consequences there will be for those who chose to violate them. Don't be discouraged as this is a huge task, and it will take some time and effort. This is why you might want to start out easy and set only those boundaries that you are willing to enforce with just one or two people, before tackling more difficult ones.

Consider this like a school assignment. When you were in school, you had several classes with teachers who gave you homework assignments. You completed them in the same night, one-by-one. This is how you accomplish setting boundaries, one step at a time, one boundary at a time. When you begin to feel overwhelmed, take a break and do something else, then go back to it later.

The next thing on your agenda is to sit down, review, and decide with whom you want to spend time or to hang out with, and those with whom you do not. Who will support you in your lifestyle change in becoming assertive? Who will be the positive support person in your life? This is the criterion I suggest you follow, which will be a difficult task, because some of these people may need to be *"kicked to the curb,"* so to speak. They might be family members, a boyfriend or girlfriend, wife or husband. If you have adult children you might have to do this with one of them. This is never an easy task. When you decide who you need to kick to the curb, you now must rehearse what and how you are going to deliver the message that identifies your boundaries with this person... then you have to be prepared to enforce them. Do not allow anyone to engage you into an argument involving your boundaries. You have a right *not* to explain why you set a particular boundary. You may simply reply that these boundaries are for the betterment of your life, and they have an equal right to either accept or reject your boundaries. It's their choice!

Here's another writing assignment that requires you to be fiercely honest with yourself. It is a really tough one, because you have to be open minded. Do not analyze, rationalize, justify, or intellectualize any of your answers. Write down what your strengths and weaknesses are within your personality, behaviors, beliefs, and attitudes. Identify weaknesses, such as the harmful beliefs you carry around with you. A strength might be that you are a hard worker, with a good work ethic, and that you are responsible. Once you have those, you might add to it later... most people do. Ask close friends and relatives that you trust, what they see in you, how they perceive you, what they believe your strengths and weaknesses are, and why. Write those down as well and compare them to your own. You will begin to see many things about your behaviors and personality that might need immediate assistance.

This is developing a self-awareness of who you are and who you want to be.

When you ascertain what personality type you are, it will help you understand what your strengths and weaknesses are, what your boundaries should be, and how to enforce them. You now are more capable of understanding who you really are. It is important to understand why you are the way you are (without pointing fingers), and what it will take to regain your identity and your individuality.

Understanding who and why you are the way you are, is a major factor in your healing process. Having figured out these things helps develop an understanding of the same information about your abuser. If you understand why a person does certain things, wouldn't it be easier to forgive them and walk away from them? Yes, you may have to walk away to achieve happiness and freedom. Disregard saying things like, *"I don't care to understand them because of what they did, etc."* I know this is hard, but if you want true healing for yourself, put away your self-pity and tackle this as if you were doing this for someone you love... Because you are, aren't you? You do love yourself, right? Wouldn't a clear understanding make it easier to develop some healing procedures for yourself? Developing an understanding of these issues will enable you to heal faster. It will also help you to understand why the abuser did what they did. You don't have to like or agree with what has happened, I certainly don't like or agree with what happened to me, but I do understand it. This has helped me to heal and to deal with all of my issues much more easily and quickly.

You now need to become focused on learning to effectively communicate, not just with others, but also with yourself. Do the internal work that is required to continue this positive process of growing and learning to give and take feedback.

Note: The negative beliefs you have developed over the years that control your feelings and emotions needs to change. If they do not, it will prevent you from moving forward and will allow you to keep living as an emotional prisoner. You will continue to live in the past on a fast track that continues to replay repeatedly.

What exactly is change? Change is nothing more than taking a risk! What risk is there in changing your negative beliefs? Fear and laziness are two commonalities that prevent us from taking the risk to change those beliefs. We fear rejection or engaging in confrontation; we are fearful of the unknown.

I am so very passionate about what I do. When I meet someone who is "stuck" and their lives are in turmoil or on a self-destructive path, I will do everything in my power to educate them. The negative past beliefs I lived with caused me to have the frame of mind that I felt I had to "convince" these individuals they needed to consider a change. Because of my passion, I became over-zealous. I felt compelled to push my knowledge onto other people to cause them to help themselves. This usually caused them to drift away, get angry, and many times people would avoid me. On examining why people were reacting to me this way, I realized my behavior was a direct result of my insecurity toward my own beliefs and lack of self-confidence. Therefore, I felt I had to convince people of my knowledge. I found that my behavior, although well intended, was extremely offensive. I didn't blame people for their reactions.

I had to decide either to blame them for being rude or to accept my responsibility in their behavior. I had influenced their negative behaviors, and I further needed to decide if I would change it or not. What would be the pros and cons of changing versus not changing? I determined that by not changing, it would be more devastating to me and would cause me to become embittered, angry, and resentful toward others. I decided to change; mind you, it was not easy. I must admit that I do slip occasionally and fall back into that old behavior at times, which is very normal. Although you shouldn't worry a great deal about it, be aware that this happens from time to time. It is my sole responsibility to be cognizant of my own behaviors and to keep them in check. It is also my responsibility to apologize when I offend or hurt someone.

My point is this… Any kind of behavioral change is difficult because it is a lifestyle change you have to work on daily. When this situation occurs, I ask myself what is it that I can control? Most generally, the answer is nothing. We only control ourselves and how people affect us. People will change when they are ready, not before. It is your personal influence, the way you act and how you treat others that creates the desire in others to change, it is *not* in your control.

ASSERTIVENESS = EMPOWERMENT

Assertiveness is your personal pathway to emotional freedom. It will help you regain control over your own life, future, relationships, and your personal success.

You have been offered all the tools and shown how to use them to create, maintain, and nurture your identity and independence to become a creative and caring individual. If practiced, these tools will enable you to regain your dignity, integrity, and most importantly, your identity…if you choose to use them.

Learning these tools and techniques will protect you, your rights, and your most valuable assets. If you give them away, it will be even more difficult to regain them later. No man, woman, child, or organization can ever take these from you, but you certainly can give them away. Do not ever give away your *"dignity and integrity!!"* In uncertain times, ask yourself if you want to be happy, or if you want to be right…

Four Behaviors to Personal Destruction ▬▬▬▬▬

I don't know of many people who do not use the following behaviors daily to some degree. They **1)** take things personally, **2)** are critical of others, **3)** deny responsibility, and **4)** don't listen. These four behaviors go hand-in-hand with two strong motivators that we talked about earlier, i.e. fear and anger. These behaviors have caused each of us problems at certain times in our lives, and will affect every relationship we have if they are not corrected.

It is important to understand as much as you can about these behaviors and how and why they work. It is tremendously difficult to examine these behaviors when they pertain to us personally. Most people are unaware they use them, but unless they are aware, they can not stop.

The subject of criticism was previously discussed, and it might be helpful to review it. There are many reasons why we criticize others. One reason is because we see something in that person we dislike in ourselves. When seeing this in others, we may get angry or create a dislike for that person. Interestingly, if we get to know that person and begin to like them, for some reason we forget, ignore, rationalize, justify, or intellectualize those flaws away, which allows us to accept them.

Another reason for our frustration or dislike comes from our moral belief system. These could be developed from your cognitive distortions, such as envy or jealousy, or from resentments we may be carrying from childhood. People are not born to be critical of others; these are learned behaviors and there are many reasons we become judgmental. It is easy to become critical because it is easier for us to examine the faults of others rather than scrutinize our own behaviors and attitudes. In other words, it is extremely difficult to come face-to-face with our own faults, and even tougher to hear about them.

An important issue that needs consideration is that many people compare themselves to others, then criticize the person with whom they have compared themselves. They justify their feelings and opinions to appear better than this other person. This act of comparing comes from a low self-esteem, little or no confidence, low self-worth, and no sense of self. Now, if someone else is comparing you to another, this brings forth anger and resentment much quicker.

When you see things in others that you don't like in yourself, you feel anger, frustration, and possibly resentment. Then you slip into denial, because you don't want to face up to your own issues. You begin thinking of those memories that caused your self-esteem, confidence, and self-worth to be damaged. These cause you to **"take things personally,"** especially if the issues are specifically directed at you. Generally, these have a direct correlation with those that originally damaged you in the first place, and can be reframed to a more positive resolution. Anger, resentment, fear, cognitive distortions, and many more, can all cause you to take things personally and be critical of others.

The feelings of **"insecurity and doubt"** cause you to have doubt about yourself and your abilities. If you have ambiguity about being a happy, healthy, normal human being, it is easy to become aggressive in your attempt to prove yourself. I was that way for years, and at times my aggressiveness grew into physical violence toward others and myself.

I would argue vehemently and even get physical at times, just to prove myself. By then, people weren't interested in listening; they just wanted to leave. The result was that I developed a reputation of being a know-it-all, a jerk, and a hard ass. My reputation was much less desirable than I wanted.

When I developed faith in God and confidence in my abilities and myself, I didn't feel the need to get angry and pushy. I didn't feel the need to *"convince"* anyone of anything. When we develop faith and confidence, we will automatically trust our abilities; we stop taking things personally and begin to respect the reality of others. I know I have said this numerous times… when you respect one's reality, you don't have to like it, accept it, or agree with it. It simply means the other person has a right to say and feel the way they want, just as you do.

When it comes to looking inward and doing a self–examination (*self-awareness*), no one likes to know they are acting or behaving inappropriately or offensively. No one likes to know they treat others poorly. People rarely admit they have the same bad behaviors as those they criticize. So, what commonly occurs is they float down the river of denial, which goes hand-in-hand with not listening.

These people prefer not to accept responsibility for their actions. They look inward and will not admit to doing or saying anything hurtful. They refuse to listen and deny any fault. If they hear these things about themselves, they may willingly do the right thing because of the embarrassment they feel.

We all know that doing the right thing isn't always easy. When acknowledged, the result is positive and is the most honorable thing to do. Let's look at teenagers; they have always been quite proficient at tuning out those they prefer not to hear, and isn't that what we do when we are forced to listen? This act accomplishes nothing.

When fear and anger set in for long periods, it is easy to get to a point where we develop an "I don't care" attitude, which prevents us from listening. This in turn enables us to jump into the river of denial, become critical, and take everything personally.

Cognitive distortions and living in the past, which are self-destructive and generally negative in nature, have a powerful impact on us taking things personally, being in denial, and not listening. All of these will affect our lives and relationships negatively. Criticism is often used as a weapon in marital relationships, at your job, raising children, etc.

Taking things personally points inwardly resulting in self-destruction, and has a direct affect on everyone around you. It will cause you to push others away and keeps you stagnated in self-pity. It maintains your anger and resentment and keeps the fire burning bright and hot. This will always prohibit you from moving forward to a healthier lifestyle.

I want to remind you again; **life is wonderful because it is a choice**. You may choose to live in pain, hurt, and resentment, or you can choose to live happy and healthy! It is your choice!

Here I Am

You're probably wondering what, *"Here I Am"* has to do with anything. Passive and passive-aggressive personality types don't want a lot of attention focused on them. If unseen, we feel there are fewer chances of being hurt or abused, and we feel safe and in control. If unnoticed, doesn't this have a negative effect on self-esteem, self-worth, and sense of self?

When you want to be unseen or unnoticed, you hide your inner-self. You cheat yourself out of knowing who you really are. The people who care about you are being cheated, as well. You cheat them out of the kindness, strength, wisdom, and love you possess. You hide and eventually kill the wonderful legacy that you have deep inside.

If you recall, one of the major needs we all have is acceptance. When you adopt these tools and allow yourself to grow and blossom, you will begin to be noticed and make a wonderfully positive statement, *"Here I am."* The subject of *"acceptance"* will be discussed at great length in my next book entitled, "Love is an Action."

I believe all people have a right to be noticed, acknowledged, and accepted. This need of *acceptance* is vitally important for any relationship you enter; it is imperative to pass these down to your children. To feel, *"Here I am,"* is very empowering.

The needs we have been discussing are not simply ideas or theories, but tools that are real gifts from God. I know some of you might not believe in God; that is your choice. I have been unable to explain who, what, why, where and how these needs came about; and therefore must assume they came from God. If they are gifts, don't we have an obligation to take care of these needs and nurture them, so we can pass them down to our children and be a positive influence for them? Be in the moment for you and your loved ones… Be real…be authentic!

How does all this relate to your Relationships?

Please contemplate this question. If you were standing in a swamp surrounded by

hungry alligators and you were bitten on the butt, how long would you continue to stand there before moving out of their reach? When you are in an emotionally, physically, or sexually abusive relationship, you are definitely standing in a swamp surrounded by hungry alligators! Sooner or later you will die emotionally and or physically. No matter how you rationalize it, justify it, or intellectualize it, you will die!

How do these tools, techniques, and concepts apply to your intimate, personal, professional, and familial relationships? Regardless of how many relationships you have, you are all *equally responsible* for the maintenance and nurturing of each relationship you enter into. In order to create and maintain happy and healthy relationships, it is important to accept the simple fact that they all begin internally with you.

There are two basic types of relationships. First and most important is the intra-personal, which is that relationship we have with ourselves. The second is inter-personal, which are the relationships we have with others. In order to create a healthy inter-personal relationship, it is important to first develop a healthy intra-personal relationship with ourselves. You have to accept <u>YOU</u> for who you really are, and you have to respect and love who you are… Does this make sense?

All of these tools, techniques, and concepts will assist you in the development of your relationships. Relationships play a huge part in our lives, and each is impacted by how we live, act, treat others, communicate, and how we set and enforce reciprocal boundaries. All these things, including what we believe, will automatically attract others of similar lifestyles and turn away those with opposing (*negative*) lifestyles.

There is a concept or behavior very common in those individuals not possessing these tools. It is a very destructive weapon to any and all relationships and lifestyles. It is used by men and

women alike and is called, *"Emotional Blackmail."* I am sure you have experienced this and may even have used it yourself.

EMOTIONAL BLACKMAIL

Emotional blackmail often occurs during an argument or fight, when one of you brings up past negative behaviors, choices, or actions of the other. It often hurts and can become a contest about who can hurt the other person the most. Believe me when I tell you this is not worth any amount of money, material possessions, or emotional pride. This act causes more resentment, anger, hurt, and horrible memories that will last a lifetime. If you haven't the tools, techniques, and concepts to defend yourself and others, then you will most likely develop negative and hurtful practices and behaviors… one of which is emotional blackmail.

Regardless of the type of relationship, all of these tools, techniques, and concepts will give you strength, courage, and the confidence to attain positive self-esteem and self-worth for yourself. With this important information, you will begin teaching others how to treat and respect you. Through this kind of lifestyle, you will have the ability to create stronger, healthier, and happier relationships; these are just the kind you want and need. You will pass this lifestyle onto your children and influence others how to live their lives in an assertive way. Relationships worth keeping need these tools to survive.

The following page is a Self-worth Assessment. If you haven't taken this assessment yet, please read each question carefully. Do not rationalize, justify, or intellectualize your answers. Put a check mark in the box next to those questions you answer, *Yes.* When checking these questions, examine your self-worth to see if you need to make some changes. If you mark any of these, there is a strong need to examine and make changes in your life. This book will help you in making those changes.

Assess Your Self-Worth ━━━━━━━━━━━━━━━━━

1. Do you routinely practice negative self-talk? ☐
2. Do you have difficulty expressing or dealing with your feelings? ☐
3. Do you feel uneasy in a social environment? ☐
4. Do you discount your successes and/or accomplishments? ☐
5. Do you get angry with yourself over mistakes you've made? ☐
6. Do you become anxious over what others think or say about you? ☐
7. Do you measure your value by serving others? ☐
8. When things do not go right, do you blame yourself? ☐
9. When you are disappointed or hurt, do you blame yourself? ☐
10. Do you place great value on perfection? ☐
11. Do you avoid making changes, taking a risk, or trying new things? ☐
12. Do you feel inferior to others? ☐
13. Do you avoid speaking your mind, thoughts, ideas, opinions, dreams and so on? ☐
14. Do you feel sad most of the time? ☐
15. In social situations, do you prefer to be a fly on the wall? ☐
16. Do you isolate from others? ☐
17. Are you fearful of authority figures? ☐
18. Do you feel a need to seek approval from others? ☐
19. Do you get angry when criticized by others? ☐
20. Do you place more value on the needs of others rather than your own? ☐
21. Do you feel as though you have no right to defend your feelings? ☐
22. Are you fearful of standing up for yourself? ☐
23. Do you have difficulty saying No? ☐
24. Do you fight the urge to cry? ☐
25. Do you believe crying is a sign of weakness? ☐

26. Have you stuffed those feelings from
    a traumatic childhood?   ☐
27. Do you deny feelings from your childhood
    because they hurt so much?   ☐
28. Do you judge yourself harshly?   ☐
29. Are you fearful of being abandoned?   ☐
30. Do you feel others are controlling you?   ☐

If you checked any of these questions honestly, without rationalizing or justifying them, then it is apparent that some work is required to bring your value up to where it needs to be. These questions are simply indicators that need to be actively considered. One's self-esteem or self-worth will fluctuate depending on the different stimuli encountered. You are looking for your core value. If you live in any of these conditions daily, then work on those specific areas. This book will help you to succeed and become the person you desire.

People usually develop a low self-esteem or self-worth from what they have learned as a child, but they can develop this at any age during their life. Possessing a low self-esteem or self-worth *does not mean you are a bad person* or that your worth is less than another. It simply means there are things in your life you need to learn so you can grow into the desired person you want to be. It also means you need to learn *coping skills*; all these things are available within the pages of this book.

We have examined in depth those areas that will help you overcome a low self-esteem or self-worth. One is self-awareness, having the desire and willingness to identify, acknowledge, and express your feelings, and to control yourself. It is also creating balance in your personal and environmental life.

Developing U.S.A [Unconditional Self Acceptance] is simply believing in "you" and learning how to effectively communicate your feelings, thoughts, ideas, dreams, and displeasures. It is utilizing the ability to say, no. It is setting and enforcing your reciprocal boundaries, defending your personal rights and giving yourself permission to accept that you are human, and it is okay to make mistakes!

Realize and accept that you have the power to accomplish anything you desire. In this book, you have learned there is very little you can control, i.e. yourself and how people and situations affect you. This is where your personal power comes in. It is important to re-evaluate your values, and create the sense of self (*self image*) you want, change those old tapes or negative self-talk into positive ones you know are true.

By developing your self-worth you become a stronger, more powerful influence on your children and others, which is a priceless gift that you alone can give. You'll be more capable of dealing with stressful situations and can manage anger more effectively, make better decisions, and increase your problem solving skills. Lastly, it will improve all your relationships and you'll be happier and more successful in life.

Inspiration

"I ASKED GOD FOR STRENGTH THAT I MIGHT ACHIEVE.
I WAS MADE WEAK THAT I MIGHT LEARN HUMBLY TO OBEY.

I ASKED FOR HEALTH THAT I MIGHT DO GREATER THINGS.
I WAS GIVEN INFIRMITY THAT I MIGHT DO BETTER THINGS.

I ASKED FOR RICHES THAT I MIGHT BE HAPPY.
I WAS GIVEN POVERTY THAT I MIGHT BE WISE.

I ASKED FOR POWER THAT I MIGHT HAVE THE PRAISE OF MEN.
I WAS GIVEN WEAKNESS THAT I MIGHT FEEL THE NEED OF GOD.

I ASKED FOR ALL THINGS THAT I MIGHT ENJOY LIFE.
I WAS GIVEN LIFE THAT I MIGHT ENJOY ALL THINGS.

I GOT NOTHING THAT I ASKED FOR, BUT EVERYTHING I HOPED FOR.
ALMOST DESPITE MYSELF, MY UNSPOKEN PRAYERS WERE ANSWERED.

I AM, AMONG ALL MEN, MOST RICHLY BLESSED."

~Anonymous~

CHAPTER **16**

Case Studies

Female Case Study #1 ━━━━━━━━━━━━━━━━━

To protect her identity, I will refer to this woman as, "Mary." This was a very long case, so I will give a synopsis of the highlight.

HISTORY:

I was in my first year of private practice when I met Mary. She called and asked if I could help her, and I suggested she come in for a free consultation. She was referred to me by another client and came in several days later. When she entered my office, my heart hit the floor. Her appearance was extremely disheveled; her hair was straight and pulled back in a pony tail, and she wore no makeup. Her affect (feelings, emotions, and moods) was sullen, her shoulders drooped, and she would not make eye contact with me. Her arms were tightly locked across her chest as she gazed at the floor. When she sat in the chair, her legs were firmly planted, as she continued to stare at the floor. She sat there for several minutes before speaking.

When she did speak, she appeared to have a nervous twitch as she bounced her foot up and down. The more she talked, the faster the bounce. It was easy to tell she had been severely traumatized.

I asked what I could do for her and with some coaxing, she began to open up and relate to me the nightmare she had been living with for 45 years.

This woman came from a rather large family; including her parents, the family members numbered 10. As she began to tell me her story, her eyes filled with tears and she began to tremble. Mary told me she wanted some help desperately but didn't know where to go or how to get it. She was also very fearful of her alcoholic husband. We talked about her options of safe houses, and I told her I would help her to get out of that situation, so she would be safe, but she had to follow through with the plans that we put together. She told me that she would have to think about it.

As she was leaving my office, Mary related to me that she had been seeing a psychiatrist, a psychologist, or some kind of counselor for 27 years and felt this was her last chance. I asked if she was still seeing someone, and she said, "yes," but my husband doesn't know about it because if he did, he'd beat the hell out of me." I explained to her that if she really wanted help that I would help her, as long as she was willing to do the work. I further expressed to her that she needed to make a solid commitment to herself and to the process. I advised her this was going to be the most difficult thing she would ever do, but that she could do it if she wanted it bad enough. I told her if she was committed, I would hold her hand through the entire process, but she must do the work herself. She shook her head and said she would think about it.

I didn't hear from her for several weeks and I pretty much dismissed it. Then one day I received a call from her; she sounded upset and made an appointment. Mary came across as an intelligent and articulate woman who had a wonderful heart but had no idea who she was. In our first session, I could tell she was determined and committed.

As she began to tell her story, I could see the pain, anger, and fear that she had locked up inside of her; my heart ached for her. From the time she was three years of age, she was sexually violated by her father. As a matter of fact, all of her siblings were violated, both boys and girls alike. She related that her mother knew what was going on but suspected it was because of fear that she did nothing to protect them. Mary added that her father had passed away a few years before she came to see me.

She stated that during and after every incident of abuse with her father, she was told that she was loved and that this was normal because this was how little girls showed their love. She also related that even after the beatings they all received, they were told they were loved. Mary learned to equate love with abuse.

When Mary was 21, she went to her mother's house to help out because she was ill. Mary was married by this time, so she wasn't concerned about her father. Unbeknownst to her, her father didn't care about her marriage and raped her on the bathroom floor. This caused her husband to divorce her.

From then on, every relationship she became involved with was emotionally, sexually, and physically abusive. All of these men were alcoholics and or drug addicts, and she was unable to hold a job for more than a month at a time.

She disclosed during one session about a room she feared in her mother's house. This was the room where her father molested her and her siblings; according to Mary, it made her skin crawl.

She commented that she would get into arguments and fights with her siblings. These arguments and fights were caused when she would bring up the painful memories of what happened to them as children. Mary stated that their family was rather close, and at the same time, it appeared they hated one another. She said that some of them were in denial about what happened. She continued to tell me that a couple of her brothers had bouts with the law and even went to prison and a few of her sisters and brothers were addicts themselves. And all of them had terrible attitudes and behaviors that were at times, volatile. She was weary of these behaviors because it was extremely stressful, and she felt it was tearing her apart emotionally.

PROGRESS:

We worked together for a solid year, and then we had periodic checkups. Mary did an inordinate amount of emotional work and worked hard in the face of her demands. She had so many issues stacked against her. She commented several times that she felt she would never make it. However, she persisted through the tears, fears, anger, and resentments and when she had seen and felt that she was making some headway, it gave her hope and strength to continue forward.

She not only learned the tools and techniques in this book, she went one step further. Mary began living them, regardless of how difficult it was at the time, and she owned them for her own. She made peace with the room that she was so fearful of. She was extremely proud the day she came in and told me she had begun to turn the room she feared into a reading room after removing the door. She said her siblings taunted her by saying that she was nuts...she was crazy. She learned to forgive herself and her mother, and she learned to accept her father for what he was and who he was. She learned to set and enforce her reciprocal boundaries. She learned to problem solve, decision make, and most importantly she regained her identity and sense of self. She learned to effectively communicate... and today, she is okay!

PROGNOSIS:

I have lost contact with Mary over the years, but the last time I heard, she was doing very well. After not being able to hold a job for more than a month, today she has worked her way up to management with 15 employees under her. She is passing on the things she learned down to her son, who is also doing very well. Further, I heard she is in a healthy relationship with someone who loves and respects her and her son. I am so proud of the courage she showed and of the fight she successfully won.

Male Case Study #2

I will refer to the person in this story as Mike, to protect my client's identity.

HISTORY:

I first met Mike while working for the Salvation Army as an Addictions Counselor; he was assigned to my caseload. The Salvation Army is a 6-month drug and alcohol rehabilitation program, from which Mike successfully completed and graduated. I have continued to work with him off and on, ever since I met him, now being almost 10 years. When he was first assigned to me, he appeared to be a beaten man. He was filled with fear, frustration, confusion, anger, resentment, and hopelessness; he was on the verge of suicide. He was into self-mutilation; he cut on himself as a punishment to others and to himself. This was the only way he knew how to deal with his life issues.

As a child, he was assaulted sexually, which added to his tumultuous existence. As he grew older, he used alcohol and drugs to deal with his issues, which led him back into cutting himself again. He was living in a horrific cycle of pain and didn't know how to appropriately deal with the things troubling him. As a boy, the most important and influential figure in his life, was his father, who told him he never wanted children. Subsequently, Mike was handed off from one family member to another, and when that no longer worked, he became the responsibility of the state. His father shared this with me personally on several occasions.

Mike was constantly told by his father that he needed to stop feeling sorry for himself, and that he needed to grow up and become a man. I know it sounds strange, but with his existence, it was important for him to understand how to do this and why. Even more imperative was for Mike to have someone to love and accept him.

As with any addict, Mike refused to recognize and accept

personal responsibility for his actions and decisions. The anger he felt for the people who violated him grew as the months and years went by and eventually spilled over onto authority figures. It overflowed onto anyone he suspected of attempting to hurt him. Ultimately, his anger spilled out onto his wife and children almost to the point of taking their lives. Mike's existence became nothing more than a life filled with hurt, anger, hate, and resentment. He was focused on blaming everyone but himself, and felt justified for those beliefs. He finally realized those behaviors didn't work for him. He was on a self-destructive track and was living in physical and emotional misery.

We are all taught how to read, write, and perform mathematical equations in school; unfortunately, most of us are not taught how to effectively problem solve or communicate with another person. This is not an excuse for his bad behaviors or for violating the law, although, no one arbitrarily decides to put themselves or others in jeopardy for no reason.

When Mike was first incarcerated, he would call me with tremendous anger in his voice. He would speak with much confusion and frustration, and his choice of adjectives was less than desirable. He blamed everyone and everything for his suffering and when asked about his own responsibility, he ignored the question or showed more anger, and sometimes both. As his anger grew, he would sidetrack the issues while blaming others. His thought processes were stunted as he primarily focused on the blame game. He was not able to move forward. If he moved at all, he moved further back into a time of more hurtful memories.

He rationalized and justified all his actions and behaviors, coming up with excuses to justify his self-destructive behaviors, his anger, and his lifestyle. By doing this, he felt entitled to continue. He possessed almost no problem solving, decision-making, or communication skills. He had extreme difficulty communicating his feelings and emotions. He told me once that he really didn't know what happiness was or how to achieve it. To survive, Mike's life boiled down to the constant use of anger, sex, alcohol, and violence.

Progress:

Through much effort, hard work, and a solid personal commitment to himself and to his goals, Mike has taken the most difficult challenge of all. He has decided to do something about it…doing something the majority of us are too fearful or lazy to do; something the majority of addicts and inmates would never consider. The pressure he lives with from other inmates and prison guards is tremendous, when factoring in his commitment, his challenge increases to a much higher and more difficult level. Mike has continued to stand strong in his commitment. Do you think people who do not live in prison would have an easier time keeping this type of commitment? I do! He has learned and does everything possible to live the information in this book. As with many of us, he is constantly learning and improving… There is light at the end of his tunnel. There is a light at the end of your tunnel, as well.

He is willfully and actively changing his life-long, negative belief patterns and his behaviors. He is learning the tools and skills needed to achieve and maintain a happy, healthy, and productive life. The most difficult thing for anyone to do is to change a negative lifestyle into a positive one, and Mike is doing it. He is slowly changing all aspects of his life. This includes changing his thoughts, beliefs, and ideologies, and his controlling, manipulative behaviors. He's learning to forgive those who have hurt him, and most importantly, he has learned to forgive himself.

Mike has learned to open his heart and mind to the sensitivities of others, as well as to his own… to be a better person. This will enable him to be a positive influence for his children and others in his world.

Specifically, Mike has been working on and continues to work on his addiction, anger management, effective communication, forgiveness, problem solving and decision making skills, assertiveness, accepting and understanding personal responsibilities and consequences, time management, life structure, and even budgeting his finances. We have also worked on job seeking skills, resume writing and most importantly, **NOT** taking things personally.

Mike is learning self-acceptance, and has learned to accept and respect the realities of others without frustration and anger. He is learning to validate his own successes without having to rely on validation from others.

Validating your own successes without relying on validation from others, mitigates the craving of wanting to be accepted by others; it creates independence and individuality. This is not to say that the validation of others isn't important, as it is absolutely essential for all of us to feel accepted. Mike knows he can continue to succeed without the validation of others, and so can you. It is wonderful to be free from feeling needy; this is independence.

Mike has created a structured plan for his transition back into society, to reduce the stress and frustrations in his life. He has learned to separate his cognitive distortions from reality and truth and has learned to do all those things he never learned as a youngster. Even though this process is extremely difficult and lengthy, he continues to do well.

Mike has finally begun to understand and accept personal responsibilities in his life and relationships. This has allowed him to begin thinking outside the box, to see the whole picture, so-to-speak. If you are too close to a situation, it is impossible to see the entire problem... i.e., *"you can't see the forest for the trees."* Thinking outside the box has enabled him to see the problems and visualize possible solutions. You can too! He is learning to analyze those solutions to ensure his success.

He is improving his problem solving skills, thought processes, and decision-making skills. It also has a positive effect on his anger management and improvement of his self-esteem and confidence level.

He is learning to be more assertive in his dealings with people, and his social skills are improving. He is teaching people how to respect him through the use of assertiveness, rather than by attempting to control people with his anger and addiction. He has learned well the important tools needed to be a productive member of society and to be happy and healthy for himself and his family. I see progress in his actions, not simply by what he says.

It doesn't stop there. I see and hear his determination for growth and success; it grows stronger each time I see him. He relates that it is because of the tools and techniques he has learned, the classes he chose to take in prison and the extra work he committed to and is still doing that is helping him become a success. As with anyone else, when handed negativity and doubt, it does have a slight problematic effect on him. However, he demonstrates his ability to effectively deal with the negativity in a more positive manner.

PROGNOSIS:

As stated earlier in this book, I believe in a concept most people have difficulty living up to called, *"Emotional Integrity."* Remember, this is *"saying what you mean, meaning what you say, and having the courage to follow through, regardless of the difficulties."*

A long time ago, I saw in Mike a strong desire to change. He didn't know how to accomplish this task and didn't have the tools, and he was fearful of the change. No one wanted to help him through this process, and it was easier for others to tell him, *"get over it,"* or *"grow up."* This is fine, except no one explained to him how to accomplish these things. People are more than willing to offer advice even when they have no idea themselves how to accomplish what they have advised. This is an ineffective way of helping anyone, in fact, it can be quite frustrating. I told Mike that as long as he continues to progress, I would never leave him until he was successful. I gave him my word, and I give it to you as well.

Mike continues to take those necessary steps to stop placing blame and pointing fingers at others. He has accepted personal responsibility for his own actions and behaviors.

The rate of recidivism in Colorado is estimated at approximately 55% over a 3-year period. The reason for this is that only a very small percentage of these individuals actually accept personal responsibility for their actions and decisions. Likewise, it's been my experience that individuals who end up returning to prison do so because they refuse to learn these tools or take responsibility for their own actions.

Because the rate of recidivism is so high, it is likely that Mike will run into some difficulties when he transitions back into society. He will need help adjusting; I have seen it more times than not. He is very much aware of these issues and has been proactive in his dealings of them as he prepares for that time and continues to request therapy. He must have a written plan in place to ensure his success, just as you will need to have one.

Mike has become very aware about making proper choices, including changing the people with whom he associates, which is part of maintaining a responsible lifestyle. It is safe to say that Mike's prognosis looks very good. If Mike continues with the momentum he has created, with the reinforcement of therapy and loving support of others, he will be successful. Mike continues to make great progress but has a long way to go.

It has taken many years for each of you to get where you are at today; and it will take some time for you to relearn and reprogram your life to be happier and healthier. I will fight to keep Mike going because I know he will succeed. I will fight to help you as well, if you so choose. I know that you can succeed, and I know your life can be what you wish to make it. What choice are you going to make today for a better future?

Thank you so much for reading this book. If you apply the above scenarios to your life, it can work for you, too. It is my prayer that the information here has inspired you to take control of your life to be happy, healthy, and successful.

YOU MUST BE ABLE, IN FRONT OF GROUPS OF OTHER PEOPLE,
TO ANIMATE YOUR TALENTS AND ABILITIES WITH YOUR SPIRITUAL FORCES,
RAISE THEM TO A CLIMAX OF BRILLIANCE IN SUCH A WAY THAT YOU
MANIFEST YOUR SPIRIT IN THE HIGHEST DEGREE THROUGH YOUR PERSON,
SO THAT YOU CAN BRING PEOPLE UNDER YOUR INFLUENCE
AND CARRY THEM UPWARD WITH YOU TO A HIGHER SPIRITUAL LEVEL.

WHEN CROWDS OF PEOPLE ENTHUSIASTICALLY CHEER AND APPLAUD YOU,
YOU MUST CONSTANTLY CARRY IN YOUR CONSCIOUSNESS
THE AWARENESS THAT THE PEOPLE ARE NOT ENTHUSIASTIC ABOUT YOUR
PERSON,
-WHICH IS ONLY AN EMPTY GARMENT BUT ABOUT GOD WHO HAS MAN-
IFESTED HIMSELF THROUGH YOUR EARTHLY INSTRUMENT.
~AUTHOR UNKNOWN~

Map Your Emotional Future

Remember the diagram that illustrated behavior on page 11? Let's see how you map out future events in your life by using that same diagram. Remember that a thought turns into a belief, which dictates how you feel, then determines your emotions, actions, and the resulting consequences of those actions.

If you have been raised with and or currently live with abuse, neglect, trauma, or other things that cause you resentments and fear, or if you possess a constant flow of negative thoughts and behaviors, these things will cause you to map out a negative future.

Every behavior you have begins with a thought...there are no exceptions. Remember the example of Tommy? He was told he was stupid all the time and the actions of his parents, teachers, and other significant people in his life supported that thought. Those thoughts then turned into beliefs. The older he gets the more negative his behaviors will become, unless there has been some positive intervention.

Choice has been mentioned in this book many, many times, but has not been discussed in the creation of behaviors. Everyone who believes in God or another higher power, knows that Jesus Christ died for our sins... but it wasn't that simple. Through that loving and selfless act, he gave all of us the wonderful and tumultuous gift of "free-will." I use the word, tumultuous, because we are fallible human beings, and we allow our poor decisions and problem solving skills to interfere with our ability to make appropriate choices. Free-will means that every man, woman, and child on this planet *has the freedom to choose how and what they do in their life.*

So, what does the development of behaviors have to do with choice? Every consistent and negative thought you have will develop and stir-up destructive feelings. When these destructive beliefs and feelings are in place, it is almost impossible to make the right choices.

For instance, if Tommy **feels** stupid, inept, worthless, and unimportant in his world, then he will make choices that support those feelings and thoughts. In a scenario like this, many of the choices he makes will be self-destructive and hurtful toward others, and some will be illegal. He might choose to use alcohol and or drugs, and run with a crowd that gives him the acceptance he craves.

He will most likely experience one or more disastrous relationships. Keep in mind that every negative outcome will add up to make the bitterness and lack of confidence increase. I am speaking from experience as I lived in this exact scenario growing up. It bled into my adult life and resulted in terrible relationships and consequences. It affected every aspect of my life in a hurtful and negative way.

Let's look at this in a more positive light. Let's say Tommy was given positive emotional, physical, and psychological support, and was told he can do anything and everything he wants to do in his life. What do you believe he will think about himself? He will likely believe he is intelligent and worthwhile and will possess a sense of belonging with a can-do attitude. These positive thoughts and feelings will enable him to make healthy, and self-developing choices. He will concentrate on becoming a success and will likely move forward in whatever field he chooses.

How does this affect those around you? Approximately 60 percent of the population are visual learners, meaning they learn primarily by what they see. This visual information is then supported by what is heard verbally, specifically by what they are told about themselves by others. This would be called criticism or feedback and can be either negative or positive.

If you are filled with hurt, anger, bitterness, and despair, these are the signals, vibes, and feelings you are projecting out to others. You are mapping out negative emotional events for your life and future. This projection is done through body language by your actions and behaviors. People see these behaviors and sense the disturbing feelings and emotions emanating from your being and naturally react in a self-protective manner. The negative feelings and emotions you project cause fear, suspicion, and scrutiny from those around you. In turn, you perceive their reactions as being offensive toward you, thus begins a vicious circle of events. Negativity begets negativity. The exact opposite is true with positive behaviors, emotions, and feelings; positivity begets positivity.

Do you realize that you expend much more energy and strength to maintain anger, resentment, and bitterness than if you concentrated on the positive aspects of your life? Negative feelings and emotions generate depression, which becomes a vicious circle of despair and carries with it more negativity, causing you to make more harmful and damaging decisions.

If there has not been any intervention and the negative lifestyle continues, as you grow older many will fall into the trap of *"living in the past."* You begin to abuse yourself with disparaging self-talk and keep your anger and frustrations at maximum destruction. This is dangerous because it can be very much like living in a whirlpool of misery that sucks you further and further down into turmoil and pain, causing more and more self-destruction and bad choices. It can explode to the point of no return. At this level of *no return*, you will refuse to listen to anyone, regardless of knowledge, education, or intent. You do this because you feel as though you don't deserve a good life, or you somehow believe it is unattainable for you. You are convinced there is no hope. You will refuse to take action to change your circumstances due to this same reasoning.

Relationships are ended, jobs are lost, drinking, and possibly drug use increases. Depression hatred, resentment, and regret become the normal way of life. The sad result is that many people give up by the time they are at this point. They feel there is no end to the misery, and they have no way out; they feel their life is worthless. This is Wrong! Wrong!! **Wrong!!!** Your life, as with mine, is a personal choice and you can make it what you desire, if you put forth the effort!

This doesn't stop at your feelings and emotions; it bleeds over into your finances, career, relationships, and every aspect of your life. The experiences that helped create the negative lifestyle you live, are not just about you. This is where the concept of influence comes in because it involves everyone you meet. Remember, no one has control over anyone; no one has control over you. However, we do have influence over others who cross our paths during our lifetime.

When looking at your past and possibly your current relationships, have you not been influenced to make poor decisions, as well as good ones? Isn't it true that the hurtful and resentful feelings and emotions you have, will dictate how you choose? You have the distinct, and absolute ability to choose how you feel, how you live, and how you want to influence others.

Do you recall the old expression, *"misery loves company?"* If you are thinking and feeling negatively, then you are likely projecting that onto everyone you come in contact with. Do you think that negativity will attract positive people? Those who are positive are the one's you can expect will support you in your endeavor. This book will guide and support you in that process.

If you prefer to have a positive, happy, healthy and wonderful life, then concentrate on that achievement. Begin thinking, feeling, and acting positively. Seek out people to assist you in achieving that goal.

Thoughts, feelings, and emotions are not simply behaviors; they result in energy transference. This is a huge aspect of influence. When you see someone in a hearty, gut splitting laugh, it becomes contagious, and you begin to chuckle, then you end up laughing right along with them. The same goes for those who are depressed, angry, and resentful. When you are around those types of behaviors long enough, you will begin to be as bitter, angry, and resentful as they. A negative lifestyle is not normal and is hard work to maintain. It isn't worth your time, life, relationships, your career, finances, identity or your sanity to continue to live with negativity.

If you are angry and tell yourself you won't get that job…guess what, you probably won't. The reason is that you not only have convinced yourself, but you have also sent out that same vibe to the person interviewing you. People intuitively pick up on that, and you set in place the destructive emotional mapping. As with everything in this book, it is not easy to change, but it is absolutely possible with the determination, acceptance of responsibility, and total commitment to yourself and your goals.

People recover from hurt feelings, and from physical and emotional abuse. It is at times difficult, but these experiences can be overcome. What makes them almost impossible to overcome is if you have experienced a severely damaged or severed spirit. This concept is an issue that is often misunderstood and overlooked.

When the **spirit** is mentioned, many people feel this denotes religion. In reality, it means strength, courage, will, fortitude, moral fiber, determination, heart, mettle, attitude, atmosphere, mood, life force, and inner-self… it is the heart of your soul. When one loses this, they are truly at the bottom.

When you go through those horrible experiences and develop a lifestyle of making poor decisions, what takes place is the deterioration of your identity. During this long and painful process, a transformation begins; your mood and attitude are affected in a negative way, which affects your confidence, strength, fortitude, determination, and your heart. When these are affected, your environment is affected by the poor choices made and by the negative associations and relationships connected with you. It will affect your moral fiber, your life force, your inner-self, and the choices you make. Whether you have lived with this for fifty years or just for a year, what's worse is living with it one more day. When will you choose to begin the process of making the right choices for yourself?

Epilogue

If you place a frog in a pot of boiling water, he will immediately jump out. However, if you place a frog into a pot of cool water and turn the heat on underneath, the frog will become accustomed to the changing temperature and eventually be boiled to death. This is exactly what happens to people who live with abuse! Abuse can come from someone else or may be self inflicted. We become desensitized to the pain, hurt, and demeaning aspects of abuse, and we slowly die emotionally and sometimes physically.

At the risk of over-simplifying, what all this boils down to is that **everything** in life is a CHOICE! In order to make healthy and proper choices, the skills in this book need to be learned and practiced.

You can choose to hurt someone for whatever reason, or you can choose to make someone happy. Ladies and gentlemen, when I say *everything in life is a choice,* I am referring to only those things that are under your personal control… Nothing more.

Why is it said that in order to appreciate happiness and joyfulness in one's life, one must experience pain and sorrow? It would be impossible for anyone to embrace and rejoice in love and happiness if they do not know what it feels like to be hurt…to feel sadness. It is to help us understand that without pain and sorrow it would be inconceivable to appreciate joy and happiness and be thankful for what we have? I believe this concept has great truth to it. If you will take a hard look at your own behaviors without justifying, rationalizing, or intellectualizing, and examine how you come across to others, I believe we would be able to see more clearly how improperly we act and how we really treat others.

If you want to see a tremendous example of this, watch the film, "Pay it Forward." By considering the needs of others and doing our best to help fulfill them, it does come back around in a wonderful way. Being kind is much easier and more rewarding than being hurtful and negative. Being nasty, mean, selfish, and harmful enables us to become self-absorbed and narcissistic and to ignore what is going on around us. It creates and maintains chaos and enables us to ignore the feelings and needs of others. This is definitely not an acceptable way to act or treat others. Without a doubt, I know you do not like being treated badly... No one does!

Final note... I said earlier that bad things happen to good people. This is true! Bad things will happen to you, nevertheless, when it does, it is not a reason to stop living, growing or looking at life as a gift from God. If you do, you will miss out on all the good things life has to offer you!

It is vitally important that you accept the fact that all hurts, pains, disappointments, and even abuses are inevitable. It is **NOT** the negative things you experience throughout your life that defines you. What defines who you is how you deal with all those things that happen to you. I have tested often and know with absolute certainty that everything I have put into this book works! It will work for you as it has worked for many, many others, as well as for myself and my wife. I am not one of those writers that merely spouts off information; I practice daily what is written in this book.

These are not merely tools you pick up periodically. These tools are needed to sculpt and define who you are and the lifestyle you choose. If you have any questions, concerns or suggestions, my contact information is in the back of this book. I will definitely get back to you.

YOU CAN SUCCEED… IF YOU CHOOSE TO!

If this book has helped you, please watch for my next book, **"Love is an Action."** It is a subsequent step to achieving a happy, healthy relationship, and it will assist you in repairing a damaged one. May God be with you as you begin your journey of self dis-covery. My intent is that this book will inspire you to move forward. I have added a poem I hope offers you more incentive to grow. Thank you and I wish you well.

Master of My Fate/Captain of My Soul

Out of the night that covers me,
black as the pit from pole to pole,
I thank whatever gods may be
for my unconquerable soul

In the fell clutch of circumstances
I have not winced nor cried aloud.
Under the bludgeonings of change,
my head is bloody, but unbowed.

Beyond this place of wrath and tears
looms but the horror of the shade,
and yet the menace of the year
finds, and shall find me, unafraid.

It matters not how strait the gate,
how charged with punishments the scroll,
I am the master of my fate;
I am the captain of my soul.

By Frankie R. Faison
Illinois Wesleyan University Commencement
May 5, 2002

"*Seek first to understand and then to be understood!*"

~Stephen Covey~

Life is Like a Puzzle

Have you ever put a picture puzzle together? I have and at times, it was frustrating, stressful, and I even got angry at times, just like life.

Think about this for a moment. When you first open the box and empty it out on the table, what do you have? To me, it was a huge mess, much as my life was, maybe even likes yours is today. I discovered over the years that a puzzle is exactly like life. The information in this book will help you to put your own personal puzzle together.

Finding the pieces in the puzzle and putting them together was at times confusing, frustrating and even stressful. I had to take time, and think about and examine the pieces. I had to look at each individual piece to try to match them up.

I found that each piece had two special identifying features, similar to our lessons in life and the information in this book. Each piece has a special and unique cut. They fit in only one place in the puzzle and they connect with other pieces in very specific ways. This unique cut also gives the puzzle strength. The more pieces you fit together the stronger the puzzle. One time I picked up a completed puzzle intact; I was thrilled.

After completing of the puzzle, you have a wonderful picture. However, if you lose a piece, any piece, you have a hole, and the puzzle becomes incomplete. Much like things in life, a missing piece will cause chaos, and much like the things in this book, you need every piece, every tool to have a complete life. When you learn and practice this information, you will have a picture of where you were, where you are at present, and where you are going.

The point is that if you go through this book, learn the information, and use it daily, you'll have all the pieces you need for success. It worked for my wife, my clients, and for me personally. I wish you well and pray you will learn. It will not and cannot hurt you, but it will make you a stronger more independent person.

Lee Braddock

Self-Awareness

Self-awareness is a huge part of becoming an assertive, independent individual. After reading your book, go through and answer these questions. These questions will give you great insight as to who you are and who you want to be.

Please do not "*justify, rationalize, of intellectualize*" your answers. Answer all questions from your heart.

Here is a short exercise in self-awareness. Consider when you get angry. You'll experience some physiological changes in your body. It's important to be able to identify these changes as they are triggers that can be detected **before** you get angry. This is the time where you have the opportunity to control that anger.

Make two lists as shown below and respond to the questions. The physiological is what you feel and where you feel it. You should be able to clearly identify those indicators.

FEELING: <u>ANGER</u>

What do you feel?

Where do you feel it?

What triggers set you off? *(Triggers are those things that set you off.)*

What do you tell yourself as you are getting angry?

HOW BEHAVIOR IS LEARNED?
(EXERCISE)

Instructions for the diagram:

Use the diagram below to back track and examine the behaviors or issues you would like to change. Fill in the blanks... Begin with the *consequences* you had. Attempt to follow this back to what the original *thought* was, then examine what *belief* came from that *thought*. Where did you get that thought, from whom, and is it valid?

Examine how this affected your *feelings;* what did you feel and where are you feeling it? Next, examine how your feelings and beliefs affect your *emotions.* What actions did you take and what where the consequences of those actions? Can you change the original thought and belief to a more accurate one? If you can, then follow it through to the final consequence. This is a simple way of mapping out how you can change your belief patterns and behaviors.

Remember, this takes positive action on your part to succeed.

BEHAVIOR
THOUGHTS   -->   **FEELINGS**   -->   **EMOTIONS**

(Beliefs)   *(Actions/Consequences)*

When you examine and gain an understanding of your behavior and the causality of your behaviors, you become **aware** of the different aspects of your attitudes, beliefs, and behaviors. You now have a choice to change the negative behaviors in your relationships; this will open up entirely new possibilities in your life.

What original thought did you have?

What negative beliefs do you have?

How do these beliefs make you feel?

How do your thoughts, beliefs, and feelings make you act?

What consequences do you experience?

Self-awareness increases your ability in maintaining **FOCUS** on your behavior.

What keeps you from being self-aware?

- Feelings of failure
- Loneliness
- Feeling vulnerable
- Physical or Emotional pain
- Personality type
- Fear
- Lack of happiness
- Ego
- Pride
- Lack of self-esteem
- Lack of self-worth
- Loss of identity

Self-awareness questions… Be specific -

1. Do you accept yourself?   ☐ Yes   ☐ No

    a) Why or why not.

    b) What changes do you feel you need to make to be success-ful in life?

2. List your strengths?

   a) List your weaknesses?

3. How can you strengthen your weaknesses?

   a) How can you maintain your strengths?

4. How do your friends see you? (If need be, ask for their thoughts. Be cautious with those who will tell what they think you want to hear. Respect their opinions.)

   a) Do you agree with their descriptions? ☐ Yes ☐ No

   b) Why, or why not?

5. List two examples of when you feel most at ease.

   a) What specific characteristics were present when you felt at ease?

6. As a child, what types of activities did you enjoy doing?

   a) As an adult, what activities do you enjoy?

7. What motivates you? Why?

8. If you had no restrictions, what would your future dreams be?

   a) What steps are you taking to achieve those dreams?

9. What do you fear most in your life? Why?

   a) Where do these fears stem from? Are your fears valid?

   b) Can you change them? If not, can you change what you feel and believe about them?

10. What stresses you?

    a) How do you respond to stress?

11. What qualities do you like to see in people? Why?

    a) Do you have many friends with the same qualities as you just described? ☐ Yes ☐ No

    b) Why or why not?

12. When you disagree with someone's viewpoint, how do you react?

    a) How do you react when someone disagrees with you?

13. List those things that prevent you from being happy.

    a) List those things that **interfere** with you having a happy, healthy life and relationship.

    b) What things can you do to facilitate a happy, healthy life and relationship with yourself?

    c) What things can you do to facilitate a happy, healthy life and relationship with others?

14. List what steps you need to take to ensure your happiness.

15. When you get angry, frustrated, resentful, or embarrassed, what do you feel? Where do you feel it, and when? Be aware of these important dynamics.

16. Everyday, write down five things you are grateful for. If by the 2 or 3rd day you are stuck, you're thinking negatively. Adjust your thinking to be more positive by focusing on what you have today not on what you do not have. A healthy mind is a positive mind.

AWARENESS IN COMMUNICATION

1. What you say is more important than how you say it.

Agree _____ Disagree ___

2. The best way for you to know that someone understands what you said, is to ask them to summarize what you said in their own words.

Agree _____ Disagree___

3. Everyone should actively listen to one another for effective listening to occur.

Agree _____ Disagree___

4. When a listener receives your oral message, almost 30% of the message is lost.

Agree _____ Disagree___

5. If your message is clear and concise the listener will understand it.

Agree _____ Disagree___

6. A person who cannot effectively communicate cannot be a successful influence.

Agree _____ Disagree___

7. The best way to make sure that you have understood what others have said is to summarize what you think they have said.

Agree _____ Disagree___

8. Responding to a speaker by means of nonverbal actions is a very important part of listening.

Agree _____ Disagree___

(Note: Eye contact, nodding, saying things like "uh-huh," let the speaker know that you are actively listening.)

9. Your oral communication skills are as important as your written communication skills.

Agree _____ Disagree___

10. You are selective as to whom you effectively communicate with.

Agree _____ Disagree___

11. You are selective as to whom you will actively listen to.

Agree _____ Disagree___

12. In order to succeed in Life, Relationships, and Career, effective communication skills are a must.

Agree _____ Disagree___

13. Assertiveness is a life-style that I can use to achieve the kind of life I have always dreamed of.

Agree ___ Disagree____

14. I have the power within me to achieve the Life-style of assertiveness.

Agree ___ Disagree ____

15. Non-verbal Communication represents 5 – 7% of all Communication.

Agree ___ Disagree ____

16. The best way to resist worry is to ignore it.

Agree ___ Disagree ____

17. Active Listening is a key to creating and maintaining healthy, happy relationships personally and professionally.

Agree ___ Disagree ____

18. Empathy is a sign of weakness.

Agree ___ Disagree ____

19. Assertiveness empowers me for success in life.

Agree ___ Disagree ____

20. Self-Awareness and Effective Communication has little to do with being an Assertive person.

Agree ___ Disagree ____

21. Processing information only involves identifying Key Words and understanding the real messages that are being sent.

Agree ___ Disagree ____

After reading this book, and have a clear understanding of its concepts, the answers below represent what you should have learned on the questions above. If you have different answers, please go back and review the information. This is not to make you feel bad or feel criticized, it is simply a guide to determine where you are in your understanding.

ANSWERS:

1. Disagree	11. Disagree
2. Agree	12. Agree
3. Agree	13. Agree
4. Agree	14. Agree
5. Agree	15. Disagree
6. Agree	16. Disagree
7. Agree	17. Agree
8. Agree	18. Disagree
9. Disagree	19. Agree
10. Disagree	20. Disagree
	21. Disagree

What does it mean to be self-aware?

Are you self-aware? If so, describe your personal awareness in detail.

Knowing that 95% of all communication is non-verbal, how are you communicating daily? Describe how you perceive your body language.

Ask people you trust to describe to you how they perceive your body language. Then compare their answers with your description. What are your conclusions?

After learning what Assertiveness really is, how does it compare to your definition?

What are the differences in styles?

What prevents you from being Assertive? Please do not rationalize or justify your reasons.

By using the rules for change, can you see how becoming assertive will add value to your life? ☐ Yes ☐ No

What would this look like for you to be truly Assertive?

How would this improve or benefit your life and relationships?

Do you actively listen? ☐ Yes ☐ No ☐ Sometimes

How would actively listening improve your life and relationships?

Become aware of how you process information. Describe the process you personally go through.

Now compare your process with what is in the text. What changes do you see that may improve your life?

What steps can you implement to reduce or eliminate worry, stress, anger, frustration etc?

How would it feel if those you talk with actively listened to you?

Effective Communications
Creating Emotional Body Armor
Setting Boundaries & Barriers

After reading your Personal Rights, list those that are important to you?

What does your current body armor look like?

What would you like them to look like?

Describe in as much detail as you can what your boundaries look like today.

Describe what changes you would like to put in place to strengthen your boundaries.

Why are these changes important to you? Be detailed.

Do you set boundaries when you are angry, frustrated stressed, etc.? ☐ Yes ☐ No

If so, what will the result be? Be detailed.

What would you like to see from setting your boundaries?

What are your steps in setting your boundaries?

Do you defend your boundaries? ☐ Yes ☐ No

If so, what are your steps? If not, why? Describe in detail?

Using Self-awareness, what do you feel and where do you feel it? Be detailed? Why do you feel these things?

If you feel stress, anger, frustration what can you do to lessen these feelings so that you can effectively enforce your boundaries?

What specific barriers prevent you from setting and enforcing your boundaries?

What can you do to prevent these barriers from stopping you from setting and enforcing your boundaries?

After reading in chapter 2 about Personality types, what type are you? **Remember, do not justify or rationalize your behaviors. We are talking about your CORE behavior, the behavior you operate on in your normal day.**

What changes do you anticipate that you are going to have to implement to achieve an assertive personality type?

Effective Communications; Forgiveness; Open Ended Questions; Giving and Receiving Positive Feedback

Do you know anyone who constantly denies or refuses compliments? Who are they?

When they deny or refuse your compliment, what do you think? How does this make you feel?

For the next week, pay attention to any compliments or positive feedback that may come your way. Make an effort to accept them without diminishing or discarding them. Be aware (self-awareness) of the feelings you experience. You may feel uncomfortable accepting compliments or positive feedback, but it is important that you accept it. DO NOT rationalize or justify it away.

When you find you are accepting compliments or positive feedback, make a note of what you said and how you felt, inside and out. Use the Assertive Record attached to help guide you. At the end of the week, come back to this and reread chapter 9. Are there one or more ways that YOU discard or diminish compliments? If so, what are they?

How do people react when you reject or diminish their compliments or positive feedback? Pay attention to their body language and facial expressions.

How do they react when you accept them?

How does it make you feel when you accept positive feedback? Do you feel guilt or shame, contentment or anxiety? Beware of how you feel about yourself inside when you accept compliments, and DOCUMENT those feelings. Do not feel discouraged or disappointed if this is difficult, it WILL get easier.

When you DID NOT accept positive feedback, how did you respond and what would have been a BETTER response?

For the next week be more aware of how you react, keep a record of every compliment by using the Assertive Record. At the end of the week, review what you have done and answer the following questions:

Who did you give compliments to? Were they mostly strangers or were they people you know?

How did you react when you gave these compliments?

Throughout the week, did it get easier or more difficult to give compliments? What did you feel as you gave compliments?

Your Assertive Record

In order for us to become more Assertive, we need to pay close attention to difficult interactions with others. This will help gain a clearer understanding of those situations that are the most challenging and the ways we could approach these situations differently.

Use the Assertive Record to maintain a record of each and every interaction.

Date: _____ Time: _____ Place: _____

Person or Situation:

Your response:

Were you Assertive, Passive, Aggressive, or Passive-Aggressive?

How did it turn out?

YOUR Feelings Afterward if Negative:

YOUR Alternative Response:

If Positive, what were they?

GIVING AND RECEIVING NEGATIVE FEEDBACK

ANGER MANAGEMENT

Is there anyone, such as family members, friends, or supervisors that give you Non-Verbal Criticism? If so, who?

With the person identified above, document one time this person gave you Non-Verbal Criticism. How did you react?

What did you feel?

What did you like about it?

How did you react?

What did you not like about it?

Who has ever given you Indirect Criticism?

How did it make you feel?

Who has ever given you Direct Criticism?

How did it make you feel?

Who has ever given you Hostile Criticism?

How did it make you feel?

Think of a time when you received Negative Criticism where it went badly. Described what happened?

Who was it?

How did you respond?

How did it make you feel?

Have you ever GIVEN negative feedback to someone? If so, who?

How did it make you feel?

How did they react?

When you gave negative feedback and it didn't go well, what could you do to correct it?

What does all this have to do with ANGER MANAGEMENT?

What does all this have to do with your relationships?

How would you use these skills of the last several weeks to improve your life and relationships?

Saying "NO" and Meaning It, Making Your Requests, CONFRONTATION, and U.S.A

When and where do you get unreasonable or unwelcomed requests? Are you at home or work? Are they from friends, relatives, or others? Who makes the most requests?

Do they ask or do they assume that you'll honor their request?

What kinds of things are asked of you?

How often do you say, NO, and under what circumstances do you say it? Under what circumstances do you say, YES, when you really want to say, NO?

Briefly describe a request you received and did not want to agree to. If possible, pick one you did not respond well to, and describe how you would have liked or should have responded.

What did you say?

How did you react?

What could you have done differently?

Describe how you would like to have responded. Think about how you could have said things differently.

Answer the same questions to future requests. This will help you to get a handle on how you react.

Pick a situation in your life in which you would like to request something, a change or a favor of some kind. Analyze your behavior.

Who is involved?

DESCRIBE the actual events and statements for each stage:

EXPRESS what you felt, what you thought:

SPECIFY exactly what went on and what went through your mind:

OUTCOME. What was it; how could it be improved?

Use extra paper if necessary.

Preparing for a confrontation:

Pick a situation that you are in conflict with and answer the following questions.

Who are you in conflict with?

What is the Issue?

If need be, re-word your problem for clarity so you can focus more clearly on the issue, and not **react** to the issue.

Think about the issue you have identified. What does it mean to you for this to be happening to you or to have happened to you? What are you afraid it might mean?

Which do you want to deal with, what the real issue is or what it means to you? What seems more appropriate to you?

What is your goal in this? Do you have more than one goal?

In the conflicted situation you described, how do you need to change?

Where would a good place be to discuss this conflict? Why?

When would it be a good time to discuss it?

Is there a risk of violence?   ☐ Yes   ☐ No

If so, what is it?

RELAX:

What can you do to remain calm and relaxed in this situation?

What part of your Body Language do you need to concentrate on the most?

How does your voice typically change in situations like these?

In the confrontation you picked, what can you do that is positive?

If there are negative consequences in your *"Analyzing your behavior,"* how can you reframe it to be a positive?

In a confrontation, do you find yourself avoiding responsibility?

                                              ☐ Yes   ☐ No

Do you point fingers and place blame?   ☐ Yes   ☐ No

If so, describe how and why.

What would a positive outcome look like to you?

What positive self-talk could you tell yourself to help you through a confrontation?

"Avoid old historical issues."

What kind of old historical issues might you be tempted to bring up? How will you stay on target and focus on the issue?

What things in your confrontation need to be clarified for your satisfaction?

What motives do you have that you want to understand more clearly in this situation?

What kinds of things make you want to counterattack? How can you prevent them from occurring?

What kinds of things can you do to reward yourself for having a successful confrontation?

Did you put your confrontation plan into action? How did it go?

What was the outcome?

UNDERSTANDING IS THE KEY TO YOUR EXISTENCE!

Effective Communications
Decision Making Skills

Pick a decision you made recently that did not turn out very well.

Did you make this decision out of anger or frustration?

☐ Yes ☐ No

Describe in detail what this decision entailed.

Using Self-awareness, remember what you felt and where you felt it. Now document this information.

Keep in mind that, "EVERY DECISION YOU MAKE TODAY…WILL AFFECT YOU AND EVERYONE AROUND YOU FOR THE REST OF YOUR LIFE."

How has this decision affected you, your life, and your relationships, thus far?

Now identify the steps that you took in making this decision.

What was your **intention** or what was the **reason** for your decision?

By using the steps for developing a good decision, how could you have made a better decision?

How do you see the outcome?

What is your process for setting your priorities? Be detailed.

Effective Communications Problem Solving Skills

Problem solving is rarely considered and seldom discussed or taught. However, the results of not being able to problem solve can be devastating to you and everyone in your environment. Answering the following questions will help you in making proper decisions.

How do you problem solve?

What is your specific process?

Describe a specific problem you have had recently.

Using the tools you have learned, how would you problem solve the previous problem.

Did you have a different result? If so, what was it?

Effective Communications
Goal Setting and Maintaining

THE GOAL SETTING BLUEPRINT

Goal setting is the only process that will assure one's success. However, the results of not being able to set goals can be devastating to you and everyone in your environment. Answering the following questions will help you in setting and following through with your short and long term goals.

STEP 1. What is your **MOTIVATION** for success?

STEP 2. WRITE your goal down.

STEP 3. IDENTIFY specifically what your Goal is

STEP 4. Create a **DEADLINE**

STEP 5. Take the details from steps 3 and 4 and make a *"step-by-step"* **PLAN**.

STEP 6. Get a clear **MENTAL PICTURE** of your goal as if it is already accomplished.

STEP 7. Back your plan with **FOCUS, PERSEVERANCE, EDUCATION,** and **TENACITY**.

STEP 8. Stay **FLEXIBLE** – Because things happen that you do not plan, you may have to alter your plans. Plan for it, Murphy's Law does exist, *"whatever can go wrong, will go wrong."* Therefore, stay flexible and go with it. You'll ultimately succeed.

GOAL SETTING SKILLS
GOAL SETTING WORKSHEET

Be Specific: (Define the Goal itself, strategies, steps, dynamics of the Goal)

Make it Measurable: (Review Points for measured Success)

Attainable: (Accountability)

Realistic: (Reasonability – is it grounded in facts?)

Timely: (Is it attainable in this time period - Flexible?)

Make four columns:

GOAL: TODAY'S DATE: TARGET DATE: COMPLETION DATE:

What are the Benefits of your Goal?

What's the Worst Case Scenario? *(Decide if you can live with Worst Case Scenario)*

What Obstacles do you foresee?

Solutions to these Obstacles:

PRIORITIZING YOUR STEPS

Make three columns:

STEPS TO SUCCESS: *(Order of Importance)*   TARGET   COMPLETION

DATE: DATE:

TIME AND PRIORITY MANAGEMENT
WORKSHEET

Define your objectives and Goals:

Document your Priorities and review them constantly:

List your troublesome Time-Stealers that enslave you:

How are you spending your time? Are you Efficient or simply Busy?

CHECK LIST FOR GETTING ORGANIZED

☐ Acquire a calendar, note pad for your "to do" lists or an organizer.

☐ Record all due dates and deadlines. Prioritize tasks on "to do" lists or 3x5 cards.

☐ Check off those that you accomplish.

☐ Select the best time of the day for the type of work required.

☐ Do harder more demanding tasks when you tend to be more alert.

◄ **IT'S YOUR CHOICE**

☐ Use "post-its" as reminders of tasks and deadlines and place them in conspicuous places like the refrigerator, bathroom mirror or car dash.

☐ The more we remember, especially in starting new habits, the more likely we are to follow through with our plans.

☐ The more we practice our new actions, the more likely they will become good habits.

CPSIA information can be obtained
at www.ICGtesting.com
Printed in the USA
FSOW02n0059250815
10218FS